3 Cheers for Teaching

A Guide to Growing Professionally and Renewing Your Spirit

Bonita DeAmicis

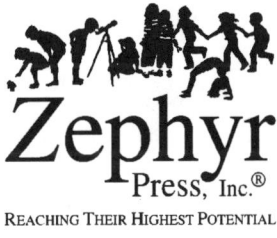

REACHING THEIR HIGHEST POTENTIAL

Tucson, Arizona

3 Cheers for Teaching

Professional Development

©1999 by Zephyr Press

ISBN 1-56976-094-2

Editors: Veronica Durie, Stacey Shropshire
Illustrations: Morgan Kent
Poetry: Kathleen Gumm
Book design: Daniel Miedaner
Cover design: Daniel Miedaner

Zephyr Press, Inc.
P.O. Box 66006
Tucson, Arizona 84728-6006
http://www.zephyrpress.com

All rights reserved. No part of this work may be reproduced or transmitted in any form by any means, electronic or mechanical, including photocopying and recording, or by any information storage or retrieval system, except as may be expressly permitted by the 1976 Copyright Act or in writing by the publisher. Requests for such permissions should be addressed to Zephyr Press.

Cataloging-in-Publication Data

DeAmicis, Bonita, 1961-
    3 cheers for teaching : a guide to growing
  professionally and renewing your spirit / Bonita DeAmicis.
      p.   cm.
    Includes bibliographical references (p.   ).
    ISBN 1-56976-094-2 (alk. paper)
    1. Teachers—United States—Handbooks, manuals, etc. 2. Teaching-
-United States—Handbooks, manuals, etc. 3. Teachers—Training of-
-United States—Handbooks, manuals, etc. I. Title.   II. Title:
Three cheers for teaching.
LB1775.2.D42   1999
371.102'0973—dc21   98-48620

This book is dedicated to Mr. Kilijanski, my fifth-grade teacher, who taught me that—

- I could write and produce my own plays, no matter how silly and incomprehensible.
- Making up an imaginary invention to solve a real problem is not crazy and may one day heal the world.
- Students who are different may have secret worlds to reveal.
- Together with my classmates I could cover the cold, hard classroom floor by sewing a classroom carpet from carpet store scraps. (The adults may have thought it ugly, but to me it was beyond beautiful.)

You may have taught to a different beat, but it is a beat that this student heard.

Acknowledgments

My thanks to the many people who helped me in this endeavor:

- Joe, Carmel, and Juliet for their continuous support and willingness to continue the household in the absence of "Mom"
- My sister, Debbie Treiber, who is my primary teacher support group
- My parents, Dorothy and Robert Johnston, for always encouraging me
- Kristi Hann for editing those very rough first chapters
- Kathleen Gumm for her beautiful poetry
- Morgan Kent for his fun illustrations
- All of the staff at Zephyr Press, in particular Ronnie Durie, for their constant support (prodding) and encouragement, and all of the other work that makes a book come to life
- And finally, Stacey Shropshire, for her beautiful editing and tireless support of my manuscript

Contents

Introduction	v
Part 1: Know Yourself	1
1. The Special Tools of a Teacher	2
2. The Heart of a Teacher	12
3. The Mind of a Teacher	27
4. The Soul of a Teacher	38
Part 2: Develop a Plan	49
5. A Teaching Ideal	50
6. A Teacher Manifesto	59
7. Self-Observation	68
8. The Habits of a Teacher	78
9. The Growth of a Teacher	90
Part 3: Take Action	99
10. Getting Started and Building Momentum	100
11. Staying on Track	109
12. Assess Yourself	118
13. Celebrate	127
14. Pass the Word	133
Resources	138
Bibliography	140

Introduction

 *Even if you're on the right track, you'll get run over if you just sit there.*
—**Will Rogers**

Why Grow?

Isn't life simpler and easier when we relax and go with the current? Once we have gone through all the work of earning our credential and landing a teaching position, we ought to be able to sit back and enjoy the ride. Doesn't becoming a teacher mean we no longer have to be students?

Absolutely! Whether you are a new teacher just starting out or a seasoned veteran, you have earned your spot in the classroom. No one says you need to extend yourself further than the textbook and curriculum requirements and an occasional "workshop" to keep your credential up to date. Nevertheless, you must understand that you have chosen a career that does not stand still. If you choose to neglect your growth you may end up overwhelmed, burnt out, and unhappy because teaching is by no means stagnant. It grows and changes in whatever ways the future demands.

Certainly a person can gain a credential and afterward teach as if working in an assembly line. We have all witnessed teachers following the assigned textbook, page-by-page, and using the precut multiple-choice-test materials to assess student progress. They attend district- or administrator-assigned staff-development courses. They passively accept any educational directives assigned by their chain of command, clients, or the political powers that be. A person can go through a teaching career in this way, function, and survive. I will not argue that doing so is not possible.

The real question is, is mere survival good enough for you? Did you become a teacher because you just wanted to survive? I'm betting something bigger brought you to teaching. My guess is that you became a teacher because something intrinsic in the act of teaching turns you on. You probably saw your role as dynamic, important, and complex. Maybe you wanted to help others. Or maybe you wanted to have an impact on the future. Why, then, after choosing and earning this career, would you be willing to cast aside your aspirations and motivations and choose instead to "survive"?

I believe you have every right to *thrive*. To thrive means to flourish and grow. It means to remain excited and refreshed by teaching. It means to go to school in the morning glad that you are a teacher and to come home in the evening feeling fulfilled and satisfied. You deserve a high quality of life! You are a teacher! You inspire the future!

Your Students Need You to Grow

One teacher was overheard saying, "Children are different today. They are much harder to handle, more unruly and undisciplined. They are not interested in learning." Another teacher responded, "Children have not changed; it is the world in which they are raised that is different."

Education is changing. It is no surprise. Everything is changing. We are in a historic period of growth unlike any we ever encountered before. Every profession, from waiter to corporate executive to engineer, requires us to continuously accommodate vast changes in lifestyle, knowledge, and technology. Every profession requires its members to grow. As educators for the future, we must not only keep pace with other professions; we very often must set the pace. After all, we are training the future employees for all professions!

To be a successful educator, one must befriend change. There are new innovations and discoveries that affect the nature of teaching: changes in knowledge and information; discovery about learning and the nature of how people learn; changes in technology, skills, and student needs. To teach means to somehow stay abreast of the changes that influence whom, what, and how you teach. It means learning and improving enough to keep up with the growth curve. If we cannot keep up, we cannot expect our students to surpass what we know, and that is exactly what we must expect them to do. Imagine a biology or astronomy professor who refuses to learn anything new. The information in that class would be obsolete in fewer than five years!

The knowledge in almost every teachable subject is expanding exponentially because of technological advances. Teachers cannot be expected to be experts in all things. Yet once again, if we are to help our students, we must at least find the means to keep pace with what we are supposed to be teaching. It is our role to know where to find the latest information. It is our role to be up to date. It is our role to lead students to the best information. In short, we must become resource managers.

Have you been following all the new information on the brain? The 1990s have been called the "decade of the brain." Current technology allows us to look inside our heads and actually watch the process of thinking. Such observation is sure to lead to explosive new ideas on the educational front. As teachers, we need to be versed in the research and its applicability in the classroom. It is certain to change aspects of teaching, but it is our responsibility to help make those changes fruitful. Our students are guinea pigs in this knowledge whirlwind. We must participate in the dialogue about the nature of learning. Otherwise, the conversation will proceed around us, and we will be left wondering where all the new-fangled teaching ideas are coming from. And we will be left wondering if our students' best interests are being served.

> *A teacher is a resource and a librarian, a partner and a coach, a measurement scale and a psychologist.*

Technology is advancing into the classroom, but teachers are not passive educational delivery systems. Computers cannot replace us. They may replace the mundane activities and skill building often associated with teaching, but they will never replace the dynamic and intuitive nature of being an educator. Computers can hold and deliver tons of information, far beyond an individual teacher's capacity. A teacher, however, can determine the wisest approach to using that information. A teacher can put the capacities of a computer to the best use based on the developmental level and needs of individual students. A teacher becomes attuned not just to the knowledge base or testing level of a student, but also to the emotional and developmental issues that make that student successful. A teacher is a resource and a librarian, a partner and a coach, a measurement scale and a psychologist. And teachers must be aware of how best to put the technological advances to work in the classroom.

Some of us wish less was required of teachers—we are here to educate; must we also be police officers, computer technicians, and social workers? The nature of how society is evolving does seem to ask more of teachers than ever before. Our students come to us with a battery of needs that go beyond our training and

Introduction

school resources. It can be frustrating and exhausting to be all things to our students. On the other hand, if we are to create learning success in our classrooms, we must acknowledge that more basic needs must be met first. We must serve as a link to services rather than a roadblock. We do not need to replace police officers and social workers, doctors and parents, but we must learn to communicate with them. We must become resources. Understanding and finding access to myriad resources on behalf of our students will make our work as teachers more fulfilling and a little easier. It will mean serving our students better. They must grow up in a world different from the one we grew up in, and we should try to grow up in their world with them.

In short, our role as educators is complex and integrated. It is no longer the world of ABCs and 123s. We are required to be higher-order thinkers. And given the direction society is heading, we are also required to produce higher-level thinkers. Rather than look upon the job as an overwhelming undertaking, it is worth our while to think of teaching as a career with unparalleled growth opportunity. You have chosen to teach. You have chosen never-ending challenge that awaits people who love the excitement and adventure of growth. Good choice!

Education Needs You to Grow

As everything around us changes exponentially, schools change, too. In fact, schools often get caught up in a whirlwind of change and adopt new methods and set new requirements almost willy-nilly to accommodate the latest political trend or appease the latest public outcry. Change can be very good for education, but teachers need to participate in the dialogue that brings about change. We work in the classrooms with students and have a unique perspective to bring to the table. The world of education needs to hear our voices. We have a role to play as advocates for effective education. We must become leaders.

Raphael Sonenshein, professor of political science at California State University at Fullerton, gave the luncheon address at the 1997 National League of Cities Conference in Los Angeles. He was asked to speak on developing a social movement for children and on the fledgling children's political movement in this country. He congratulated everyone present for supporting a worthy cause, our future, but then went on to say that the campaign falls short in a few essential areas.

One such area rang out to me. He spoke of how the children's organizations, made up of community activists, politicians, and youth themselves, often neglect two important voices: the voices of teachers and the voices of parents. These two groups, Sonenshein argued, are the most passionate groups who have invested in the lives of children. Teachers and parents are fanatical about the needs of children and can provide the real momentum any social agenda needs. The problem with the children's movement is we often spend more time recruiting agency directors, political bodies, and youth rather than passionate advocates. Teachers and parents spend their lives working to benefit youth and children, yet they are often overlooked as voices in the political arena.

> **Become informed and participate.**

When I was first considering becoming a teacher, I took a career aptitude test. It was one of those computer-operated surveys that takes your priorities, strengths, working characteristics, and so on, and compares them with those of other people working in various areas. I was a well-defined match with teachers except for one area—creativity. On the whole the survey found that teachers believed they had little influence or power over the creative aspects of their work, whereas I wanted a creative career. I felt very confused by this incongruity. "How could teachers not believe teaching to be a creative profession?" I wondered. "It has to be one of the most dynamic jobs that exist." I felt teachers must be overlooking some key aspects of their career. Perhaps they didn't see the dynamism inherent in the job.

Once I began to teach, I started to understand why teachers feel their jobs do not require creativity. Often in both national and local education debates, teachers are treated as incidental aspects of the educational process. How often have educational decisions been made without the voice of working teachers as part of the decision-making process? If the curriculum is correct, if the testing is proper, if the student population is adequately motivated, then education will succeed. Teachers must do it this way, or teachers must do it that way.

When the public demands school change and accountability, teacher voices need to be informed and clear: "This is what we think will work; this is what we know will not work." Without our participation in the discussion, schools are sure to be tossed back and forth between political agendas that have little to do with what actually happens in a classroom. The California phonics debate is a perfect example of teacher voices left out of the struggle. Almost every teacher I speak with claims the answer to teaching reading falls somewhere between phonics and whole language because children vary and have different learning styles. Many wonderful teachers have been successfully blending both methods through the years of debate. Why, then, is the argument always either phonics or whole language? Perhaps those successful teachers could have changed the nature of this discussion.

Become informed and participate. Teachers are needed as part of the national dialogue on education. We might even need to invite ourselves into it. As one mother put it, "I was thinking someone should really step up to the plate and do something about this. Then I realized . . . I am somebody."

Introduction

> **Teaching is both an art and a science.**

How to Grow

Great teaching cannot be relegated to a formula. Measurable, observable practices exist that we can use to improve and critique our teaching performance. However, in the final analysis, there are qualities that go beyond that which can be so easily defined and discerned.

Teaching is both an art and a science. We can look at art from a scientific perspective and see that there are definable elements to great art. There are scientific properties that can be applied to the way a color is mixed and displayed. We know a certain kind of balance must be achieved for a composition to work. Yet no one would disagree that there is also a quality in art that goes beyond the formula. It is unique and personal to each artist and must be accepted as such.

We are in an era of great growth in understanding of education and the nature of learning. We know students learn more successfully when given the opportunity to arrive at their own understandings in their own ways. We know cooperative groups reach more students in a more productive manner for learning. We know teacher feedback is an important ingredient for student growth. We know the human brain is built to respond to novelty and variety and likes to build its own patterns and sense.

Many of us can also name at least one great lecturer from our past, one teacher who stood up front, in that tiresome, old-fashioned way, and captivated the entire room. Most of us can remember one teacher who inspired us to read a great piece of literature or to concentrate on the complexities of the human condition or to ask the big questions without using any of the methods described previously, using instead paper-and-pencil tests.

Am I supporting a return to the podium-wrought, multiple-choice teaching methods of the past? Hardly. I *am* arguing for the recognition that teaching is complex and individual. That while we may be able to identify and promote successful teaching strategies and practices, we should not do so to the exclusion of the teacher's style and individuality. Teachers bring something to the table that is unique and indefinable. That is what makes teaching an art.

Educational Reform and Teacher Professionalism

Educational theorists, researchers, and administrators put great emphasis on systemic change. Books, materials, and consultants abound that offer systemic change and educational reform to any district or school whose leadership is interested.

William Glasser (1993) discusses some ways real change must be built into the structures, policies, and operations of the school and school system. He emphasizes that most teachers will be unsuccessful in "Quality School Theory" unless they have the support of the system itself.

As most educators can attest, support and policies of the school do affect the quality of teaching one can provide. However, a top-down focus on educational reform often leaves teachers on the sidelines, frustrated, waiting for their districts and schools to recognize the need for change. In other cases, districts and schools adopt reform measures in whatever order fashion dictates, leaving educators reacting to and dependent upon the current political movement.

Ultimately, districts and schools must be on board if we are to implement educational reform successfully. Nevertheless, we should also remember teachers all over the world have accomplished a great deal even in the most mundane and unresponsive school environments. Teachers have the power to influence change from the bottom up and should be encouraged to do so. I believe real progress in educational reform is best achieved when we build from both ends of the bridge, when schools and districts implement systemic changes that adopt reform measures in their truest workable form, while, on the opposite side of the chasm, individual teachers make individual strides toward excellence in their own classrooms.

Planning Your Professional Growth

One of my close friends is dead against self-determined professional growth. "It leads to sloppiness. You will miss something important if you follow your instincts instead of a predetermined educational course load." It is easiest and at first glance seems more direct to take the recommended educational courses at a recognized educational institution in the recommended order. You probably followed such a format to become a teacher in the first place. I'm sure the assigned battery of courses all apply to what you do as a teacher now. However, now you are working as a teacher and your time and energy for professional learning is more limited. It may be that courses designed by an educational institution or your district and offered in a predetermined order are exactly all you need. Or it may be that a higher degree, complete with all the assigned courses, is exactly what you want. More often than not, however, the courses are designed to meet the general criteria, not your specific situation. Staff development courses usually reflect district or school needs and priorities, not necessarily your most pressing needs and priorities. Certainly the classes are there for you to take advantage of; I suggest only that they should be the *starting point* for establishing professional growth priorities.

Introduction

Power and influence over your career is what I advocate. It begins with self-determination and is complemented and assisted by the resources available to you, not the other way around.

People who leave their destinies in the hands of others are often unhappy. Popular literature as well as the science of motivation tend to agree that people who feel they have a level of power or influence over their lives are happier and more satisfied. It turns out human beings are not built to sit in the waves content to be washed back and forth with the tide. We are built for action. We grab surfboards and meet the tide head on. And though we may not have power over the ocean itself, we certainly do have power over the length, breadth, and thrill of the ride.

I challenge all of you to make the ride your own. Be proactive in determining your future. You will most definitely be affected by the mood of the ocean, the political winds that drive the tide, and the ideals of your school administrators, but within that ocean it is entirely possible to design your own path. Choose to become a leader over your destiny and perhaps influence the destiny of education in the process.

Creativity vs. Planning and Preparation

You might ask, "What about spontaneity? If I take on all this planning and professional growth responsibility, won't I lose my flair for teaching? Won't I be dragging all my aspirations down with all that boring, overwrought planning?"

The "simplify your life" movement was born out of the frustration of overplanning. Creative people are prone to become boring automatons under the direction of a thick daily planner. Choosing not to plan, though, has equally damaging prospects. You may not want to be a boring automaton, but do you want to be a flighty flake with few real accomplishments? Balancing planning with creative spontaneity is the key.

Planning for professional growth doesn't work when it is too confining and too strict. It works best when it is used as a guide and complemented with freedom. This book does not promote day planners and massive to-do lists. The methods I promote should not take over your every move. I could not survive under those conditions, and I would not visit them on someone else. Instead, these methods will allow your best self to come through. The system I recommend balances the wonder and spontaneity of creativity with the purposefulness and achievement of planning.

I challenge you to know yourself better and become aware of your leading passions without confining every teacher decision you make to a set of strategic agendas. Likewise, I challenge you to experience the joy of freedom to follow your instincts, without ignoring the need for planning. The bigger part of this book is devoted to the process of self-awareness because it is there that you will find the energy and excitement that leads to real growth. The professional growth planning that you will do as you proceed will be more like keeping mental notes and general guideposts than day-to-day, play-by-play planning. Yes, you will create lists, but they will not be used as daily, monthly, or weekly agendas. Your lists will remain in a file as reminders when you feel lost or in need of a refresher.

In fact, the very first and most important area you will address in this process of self-planning is your driving passion, the thing or things that make you motivated and excited. These things are the parts of your teaching that most need to be heard, developed, and respected.

With each step taken in a self-designed professional development program comes esteem about what you do and your influence over your destiny. You feel good about teaching because you have power over the choices you are making as a teacher. Choosing to grow professionally means continually tapping into the very emotions that first led you to this career. It means building upon that original energy and thriving as a teacher because of the choices you make about your own future.

The Power of Flow and the Autotelic Personality

Mihaly Csikszentmihalyi (1990) is an innovative researcher in the psychology of human experience. His primary area of interest lies in "optimal experience." What he attempts to study and put into quantifiable terms is the nature of life fulfillment. He believes he has discovered a number of elements that are necessary to achieve life happiness. In *Flow*, he discusses how people arrive at experiences of exhilaration in their work: "A sense that one's skills are adequate to cope with the challenges at hand, in a goal-directed, rule-bound action system that provides clear clues as to how well one is performing. Concentration is so intense that there is no attention left over to think about anything irrelevant, or to worry about problems. Self-consciousness disappears, and the sense of time becomes distorted. An activity that produces such experiences is so gratifying that people are willing to do it for its own sake, with little concern for what they will get out of it, even when it is difficult or dangerous" (71).

Many teachers have felt such a moment in the classroom. The moment where the time has flown so fast that as the bell rings, neither you nor your students can believe the school day is over. Perhaps you were lost in a classroom drama project or a team debate. Perhaps you were reading literature, solving a difficult math problem, or learning to draw. Can you argue that if most days were like that one you would be the happiest teacher you could be?

Introduction

As Csikszentmihalyi describes it, flow is like playing one of those video games that moves the challenge up one notch each time you meet a challenge. It is very addictive to be involved in such an activity, as witnessed by the millions of video game parlors in malls across the United States. That same sense of exhilaration can be had in the middle of a highly competitive sports event or when getting lost in the reading of a fabulous book.

> *The ultimate responsibility for what you achieve as a teacher is in your hands.*

Flow is most often achieved intermittently in response to specific activities such as a challenging project or game, but there are also people who manage to achieve flow regularly in their day-to-day existence. Optimal experience can be described as finding joy and challenge in what you do. People who often reach the level of flow in their work are motivated, fulfilled, and happy with work. The main purpose of this book is to help teachers feel they are optimizing their experience as teachers.

Csikszentmihalyi believes happy, fulfilled individuals have learned to apply a sense of flow throughout their lives because they live by certain principles He calls these kinds of people "autotelic" and explains that we can all successfully learn and apply what they do naturally.

Flow cannot be simplified into a prescriptive formula, but it is clear a number of elements need to be active for an individual to achieve optimal experiences in work, to become autotelic:

1. Set goals: Autotelic people learn to make decisions and choices. They decide what challenges to take on and which to sidestep. They set their own agendas.
2. Become absorbed: Autotelic people select goals just above the level they are currently at, so a sincere level of challenge is required to achieve the goal, which keeps them focused and attentive on what they are striving to do. If they want to improve their reading and begin with *War and Peace,* for example, they will be unable to concentrate at the level required and will be knocked out of flow. Likewise, if they are able to read and choose only basic primers, they will become bored, which also destroys concentration.
3. Focus attention: Autotelic people give attention to what they attempt to achieve. They do not allow external influences to determine their level of attention. They are not easily distracted.

4. Find joy: Finding the enjoyment in what they do appears to be essential to the flow experience. While joy is somewhat inherent in the activity, it is also dependent on the attitude of the individual toward the activity.

Autotelic people strive to produce those above responses as a day-to-day way of living. People who achieve a lifetime of flow strive to follow these principles and direct themselves toward a lifetime purpose. They find a meaningful goal that they can address in their life's work and they develop reachable challenges to achieve that goal. This book aims to help you become an autotelic teacher. I believe if you use the tools and follow the exercises in this book, you will successfully begin to incorporate flow into your life.

Good luck. Proceed. Remember the ultimate responsibility for what you achieve as a teacher is in your hands.

A Book for Teachers

This book is written for teachers. I want teachers who read this book to feel confident and clear about their purpose and priorities as teachers. I want them to define themselves and create a blueprint for professional growth that works within the strengths and the limitations of their professional environment. I want them to create personal goals and objectives that recognize and give voice to the science and the art of teaching.

> *Self-defined, self-reflective teachers will be allies, assets, and potentially leaders in the challenge of systemic change.*

This book promotes self-reflection side-by-side with planned growth. It prepares teachers to say, "This is who I am as a teacher and this is how the school and district can support me in my endeavor to be the best teacher I can be." It prepares teachers to be professionals and leaders in the educational debate.

For a lucky few teachers, the activities will mean defining themselves in light of reform measures already taking place in their schools or districts. However, for most teachers, reading this book will set them on an independent path. These self-defined, self-reflective teachers will be allies, assets, and potentially leaders in the challenge of systemic change. Schools and districts that later elect to pursue educational reform will be fortunate to have these self-determined teachers as part of their reform efforts. Schools that do not pursue reform likewise will be blessed with professional, confident teachers.

Introduction

What to Expect

Do you strive to be the best in teaching? Do you want to feel good about what you bring to the classroom, to know that your teaching is effective? Do you want to keep your passion for teaching alive while constantly growing and improving? This book is filled with exercises and strategies for your growth. Unlike many educational resources, these activities are not for teachers to use on their students. These exercises are for you, the teacher. You may do them alone, with a partner, or with a group of peers.

The message of this book comes from a quotation attributed to Socrates, "Know Thyself." Socrates believed in asking questions and in self-discovery. In this book you will find a series of fun, thought-provoking self-discovery exercises. Your self-discoveries will become personal guideposts on your journey toward professional fulfillment.

This book is also about strengthening your belief in yourself as a teacher and your abilities to teach well. By strengthening the connection between who you are, why you teach, and how you teach, your future as a teacher will be continuously successful, fulfilling, and challenging.

Part 1: Discovery and Inspiration

Part 1 lays the groundwork for continuous professional success and fulfillment. These chapters are filled with exercises to inspire and invigorate you, and to identify the unique gifts and personal value system that you bring to the classroom. When you finish these chapters, you will feel confident that you know why you teach and what teaching qualities you should nurture and protect.

Part 2: Growth and Planning

Part 2 is about planning. You will use your self-discoveries from Part 1 as guideposts to prioritize and plan your own professional growth. You will set goals for learning and improving specific aspects of your teaching self.

Part 3: Success and Celebration

Success can feel elusive if you do not have a way to assess your progress and celebrate your growth. How are teachers presently assessed? Test scores? Principal reviews? Peer reviews? These methods of evaluation give only partial and sometimes very limited insights. Part 3 encourages another strategy: self-designed methods of assessment.

A Brief Word about Research

This book is a self-reflection and goal-setting book. Many of the ideas are drawn, adapted, and combined from goal-setting, time-management, and self-growth literature. At the end of the book is a list of resources and an index of research that supports self-reflection and goal setting, but not necessarily the specific activities proposed in this book.

The Approach

Go through this book in any order you choose. Try some or all of the exercises. If any do not fit your style or thinking, cast them aside. This book is your helper, not your master. You are special and individual. Make this book work for you.

I Chose the Sun

I chose the sun today
instead of bed
I chose the sound of water
running, the tea kettle whistling
the sight of myself in the mirror.
I chose an argument with my teenage daughter
a cold glass of grape juice, phone calls, scrambled
eggs, and a hug from my ten-year-old.
Because I was awake
there were small cradles of fear
I chose not to rock
moments of indecision
feeling I couldn't feel
There were thoughts of you—
I took a walk to the neighbor's. I curled my hair.
Found a handful of feathers in the garden, let
a sparrow out of the garage—
I don't know how long he'd been trapped
in the dark, all alone.
At first he didn't want to leave but I waited.
I waited until he found his courage
flew out and into the sun.

—Kathleen Gumm

Part 1

Know Yourself

1
The Special Tools of a Teacher

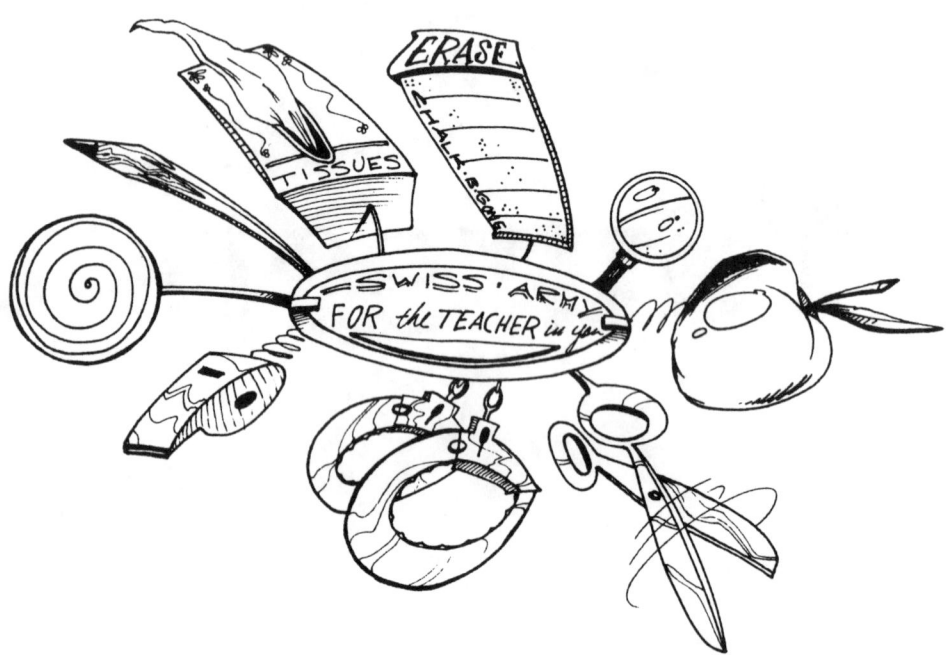

There is no one out there to tell us, "Here is a goal worth spending your life on" . . . each person must discover ultimate purpose on his or her own . . . Self-knowledge—an ancient remedy so old that its value is easily forgotten—is the process through which one may organize conflicting options.

—Mihaly Csikszentmihalyi

The Special Tools of a Teacher

This book is part inner journey, part outer practice. In this first section, we begin the inner journey. These initial chapters will take you through a series of activities that encourage self-reflection. The revelations and information you gather will serve as the launching posts for the professional development projects. To best carry out the exploration of your heart, mind, and soul, this chapter gives you special tools for the journey.

As you work with the tools described in this first chapter, understand that their ultimate purpose is to help you know yourself. Sometimes they may uncover conflict and frustration that you had not realized existed. Other times they may offer you the solace of deep personal understanding. At the very least they will make you think. I am convinced the most important work you will do with this book lies in the pages of this chapter, but only if you do the work.

Understand this book is about change. It is about growing in strength of self and becoming the best teacher you can be. Starting from the inside out will ensure that you have chosen an ideal destination for your journey.

It is in this chapter you learn about three tools that can make your self-reflective journey sparkle. These teacher tools are not what you might expect: no overheads or chalkboards, no special computers or calculators. No, the tools I recommend cost little or nothing and are easy to acquire and use. You may even already be using them in one form or another. These tools make self-reflection exercises more potent and ultimately more satisfying: a display space, a personal notebook, and a teacher support group. The more you choose to use these three tools, the more you will magnify your learning, your enthusiasm, and your commitment to the process of professional growth. The magic is simple. Anyone can read a book and think about it. Some of us may even change as a result of what we read and learn. However, most people must take it a step further to truly benefit from ideas they read. A deeper level of remembering and understanding occurs when you choose to process ideas instead of simply pondering.

> *A deeper level of remembering and understanding occurs when you choose to process ideas instead of simply pondering.*

Processing means to change a thing, to act upon it, to transform it and make it yours. You can look at a chocolate cake and appreciate it. It looks like it will taste good. You might even have the sensual imagination to taste the rich icing through your eyes. But most of us agree that taking a bite with a glass of milk far exceeds the experience of just staring and wishing! Once you take that bite, you have changed the cake and the cake has changed you (through a luscious taste sensation and more than a few calories!).

Part 1: Know Yourself

> **The three tools I recommend will change the nature of your self-exploration.**

The three tools I recommend will change the nature of your self-exploration. Your discoveries will become more far-reaching, more personal, and have a greater impact. In fact, if all you choose to do from this book is to design a display space, write in a notebook, and begin a support group, you will have taken the largest strides in an effective, fulfilling professional development journey.

If implementing all three tools seems like too much for your busy teaching schedule, I understand. But choose at least one and stick with it. Your experience will be so greatly enriched that you will not regret it.

Display Space

Find some space in a room where you spend time. You could use the walls of your home office or behind your desk at school. You could tape messages on the glove compartment of your car or on your bathroom mirror, or claim the refrigerator door as your personal mural. You might program your computer screen saver. You might even pick three or four such locations and use them all.

The main idea is to choose a space you look at at least once a day. It needs to be the kind of space where you will find yourself staring when you have run out of words or are tired from the day's activities. It is in this space you want to post information that you want to keep on the forefront of your mind. Here are two activities to get you started.

▶ *Exercise 1:*
Inspiration

Start by posting a powerful quotation or visual cue that makes you feel strong and positive. I have a passage from Nelson Mandela's 1994 inaugural speech on my office wall: "Our deepest fear is not that we are inadequate. Our deepest fear is that we are powerful beyond measure. It is our light, not our darkness, that most frightens us."

Perhaps you would rather have a photo of a triumphant moment in sports. Or maybe you feel strongest when you laugh hardest. Post your favorite Far Side comic strip or one of those wonderful *Reader's Digest* stories that can repeatedly make you smile. Find one main thing that gives you an emotional lift, a solid foundation, or a heartfelt fire and put it where you see it every day.

▶ *Exercise 2:*
Collage

Create a collage that says "You"—things that interest you, dreams you have, a picture of your fantasy life, teaching goals, moral and ethical beliefs. Words that describe you, places that are special to you, people you love. Think of the collage as a snapshot of yourself. Use it as a statement of identity. Look at it and say, "Me!"

When you are reading the morning paper or listening to the news, cut out or jot down things that catch your eye, things that inflame you, things that excite you. Cut out pictures that you like. Write down quotations or jokes or whatever strikes your fancy. Look for things that you want to know more about, and so on. Paste, staple, or tape these things onto your display area. Make it random or organize it. Give it borders and captions or let it just grow like an amoeba on the board.

Think of your display area as a return to your teenage bedroom. Remember how you hung posters of your favorite athletes or rock stars, pictures of your closest friends, snapshots of animals you loved or places you wanted to visit? Give yourself permission to allow all your different interests to shine through.

Personal Notebook

The notebook is for words and doodles and pictures and scribbles and lists. I am not talking about lecture notes or copying. This notebook requires the kind of writing where you add yourself. It will transform mere ideas and thoughts into promises and results. Somehow, the act of putting it down changes everything. You may call it a journal or a learning log, a scribble zone, or your confidante.

Get a notebook. It is best to use a three-ring binder, but you can use scraps of paper and a manila envelope, a scrapbook, or a spiral notepad. It is entirely up to you. It helps if it is something that you can comfortably bring with you, but it is not necessary. You can also carry a small notepad and transfer information or staple notepad sheets into your main notebook. If possible, put labeled dividers in your notebook so you can easily retrieve your notes. Perhaps you want to get started first, then move papers around and add the dividers later. The notebook could be a close reflection of your priorities. If you'd rather start with some dividers, try these labels to begin: 1. My morning pages; 2. Responses to self-reflection activities; and 3. Lists.

Throughout this book you will find ideas on how to use your notebook. There are no rules. You may draw or write or paste or glue or staple. You may use color or not. You may think of it as a continuation of your display space. Primarily, you want this notebook to be a place where words and pictures and ideas can work their magic. Here are two activities to start your program.

Part 1: Know Yourself

▶ Exercise 3:
Putting Down the Words

Julia Cameron (1992) recommends folks wake up ten minutes early every morning and write stream-of-consciousness thoughts. A daily stream-of-consciousness exercise can be a valuable tool in our efforts to better know ourselves. If you generally wake up at 7:00 A.M., wake at 6:50 A.M. Or if the morning doesn't work for you, try it right before you sleep. The only problem is sometimes the mental release charges you with a creative burst and you stay up all night! You can also try it at lunch, or dinner or recess break. Or require your entire class to join you on this venture and have a classroom SJT (silent journal time). Choose what works for you, but get started. Once you are doing it every day, you might be inspired to try it at different times of the day to see if you respond to the exercise differently. If you miss a day, don't give up. Start again the next day.

At the beginning of the time, go straight to the pad and pencil. Write whatever comes to mind. I often start with complaints about morning and my need for caffeine. If your thoughts end midsentence and your brain begins another line of thinking, let the words end midsentence and follow that next line. Do not erase, edit, cross off, or start over. Just write and write and write. Quit after ten minutes or three pages. Do not read back over anything you write. Just put the words down, then close the notebook. Do this exercise for more than two weeks before you go back to read over your scribbles. As you continue, don't read the pages for a few weeks. If you read what you write too soon or too often, you begin to influence your willingness to let your subconscious mind do the talking.

I had a friend say this practice was crazy. She had nothing to write down.

"Write that down," I said.

"What?" she asked.

"Write, 'I don't have anything to say this morning. This is a stupid idea. Who is this creep recommending this crazy idea? What can I possibly gain from this? My sleep is precious to me. Please let me go back to bed. What is it with this touchy-feely garbage? I am not like this. This is too impractical. Life stinks. Why am I doing this? My dog is whining. Who are those kids already out playing at this hour in the morning? How come my husband is asleep while I'm here trying to better myself? Doesn't he need to better himself? I hate this I hate this I hate this...'"

I called my friend after three days. "How are the pages doing?"

"I'm still complaining," she answered.

Three more days went by. "So, how are the pages?"

"Same." (I could here the strain in her voice.)

Three more days passed. I asked again.

"Well, a few other things are creeping in."

After a few weeks she had a chance to go back to read her pages, and in the pages was a wonderful poem that she did not even remember putting down.

Does this happen often? Perhaps. Perhaps poetry is not what is meant to come from your pages. In mine I sometimes uncover poems, but more often I clear the air, detoxify my brain, and plan for the future. Sometimes I hash through things that are upsetting me. Then, the next day my confidante the notebook gives me the solution to my problems. It is my counselor, my creativity manager, and my to-do list (when I am writing and duties cross my mind, I just jot down a note at the top of the page, then go back later and retrieve the notes for my actual list).

You must be wondering, "Do I do this for the rest of my life?" I recommend committing yourself to writing pages four of seven days a week for at least two months. After that you will probably start and stop often, but find yourself returning to the pages whenever your life seems unclear and confusing, or you just want to reconnect.

▶ *Exercise 4:*
Questions

Have you ever been around a preschooler? Ever notice how they go crazy with questions? Everything is followed by a "why?" Preschoolers' minds are capturing information at an amazing pace, and it is no accident that their active minds are filled

> **Use your notebook to reenergize the three-year-old mind lying dormant in your brain.**

with questions. Use your notebook to reenergize the three-year-old mind lying dormant in your brain. It is a great place to jot down questions that enter your mind. Anytime a question crosses your consciousness, write it down, whether it relates to your activities or not.

Questions are the backbone of any learning, and by giving your questions expression and rein they will come at you more fast and furious than they have in a long time. Consequently, you will be aware and open to finding answers. Consequently, you will be primed for learning. You have my solemn oath that you do not have to seek answers to all the questions you write. Let them stew. They will ignite better and better questions, and before you know it, your subconscious will set to work on finding the answers you need. I find that often, after I have recorded a question, I somehow meet an expert who can answer my question. Synchronicity is a strange creature and chooses to work in your life only if you invite him in.

Part 1: Know Yourself

> ***You will be amazed what a child can teach you about asking questions.***

One way to ignite questions is to sit in one room or take a short walk. Dedicate 10 minutes to asking as many questions as you can muster about your surroundings. Providing this timed, tight focus will help kick start your ability to notice and wonder about things. You can also kick start your question engine by spending some time with a three-year-old. If you don't have one of your own, go visit a friend. You will be amazed what a child can teach you about asking questions.

Another option is to read through the morning newspaper or a nonfiction article in a magazine. Cut out or copy portions that spark your interest. Paste them in your notebook and write in the margins questions that are left unanswered in the article.

Support Group

This tool works well particularly if you are an interpersonal thinker, if you like to work in groups and you enjoy camaraderie on projects. Many of the activities in this book you will do independently, and you can go through most of the book without involving others. But by forming a partnership or learning network, you create another place to process your learning and ideas, and you will have a support network in place to cheer you on, offer suggestions, and share in your successes.

The best possible kind of teacher support group would be a group facilitated by a trained group leader working on educational reform in your district or at your school site. Such a group is ideal for growing and processing. If you are lucky enough to be given such an opportunity, grab on and enjoy.

The next best choice is starting your own group or partnership. Just any teacher or just any group won't do. Use your staff room lunch crowd as your reflection group if it is filled with teachers who teach on the cutting edge, who are ready to grow and love their work. If you have such a crowd at your workplace, lucky you! If you don't, try to find just one teacher who is into his or her work, who would enjoy a once-a-week appointment with you. The partner does not have to teach the same subject you teach. You can also meet some place other than at school.

No luck at your work site? Try advertising in a teacher newsletter or publication, join a local teacher organization, or check out teachers in training at your local college. You can meet by phone, letter, or Internet. Some teacher sites on the Internet are included in the resource pages of this book.

Think of the person or people you are looking for not just as a partners in completing the exercises in this book but as a support network to help you grow and advance in your teaching. Be sure your partner or partners are people who want to grow and are happy about your decision to grow. They do not need to be just like you; the more variety in thinking the better.

Look carefully and cautiously before committing to a partnership or group. You do not want members who wish to compete with or impede the progress of others. Nothing is worse than a partner who wants to pull you down, stop your progress, or criticize your dreams. A professional facilitator may help a cynical person with a negative attitude to appreciate strengths and the importance of positive group interaction. Trained facilitators have some measure of experience with various kinds of group members. In the more informal group, it is best to leave out folks with an ax to grind or a negative attitude about teaching, learning, or support groups. Their personal issues may slowly infect the group's progress.

Here is what you say or write in your advertisement: "I'm looking for a teacher partner, someone who is interested in working with me or in a small support group. We would meet once a week or once every other week, by phone, Internet, or in person. At these meetings we would discuss our teaching styles and interests, our teaching strengths and weaknesses, our personal aspirations. We would map out goals and talk about successes. The purpose of our meetings would be to share our disasters and triumphs in teaching, to encourage goal setting and growth, and to celebrate success. If this sounds good to you, let me know."

Once you have your partners, plan a way to meet regularly and discuss the activities in this book. You should feel that you can move through this book at your own pace but that your regular meetings are a chance to review where you are and what wonderful revelations you have experienced. If you are proceeding slowly through part 1 and your partner has plowed on to the next section, that should not be a problem as long as you are supportive of each other's progress.

Here are two activities to get you started.

▶ *Exercise 5:*
Ground Rules

The first time you meet with your support group, determine the following ground rules, even if you are working with only one partner.

1. How long will meetings last? If the time commitment is not set down, you and your partner may find yourself repeatedly canceling because you don't think there will be sufficient time. Decide up front how long is appropriate and stick to your decision.

2. What measures will you take to keep one person from monopolizing the conversation? Monopolizing the conversation is not usually intentional. People can become excited as they begin to self-reflect. Also, some individuals need to talk in order to think. You could set a timer and have a limit, or pass a ball that the talker holds as a physical reminder of the time he is using. It is important to be sure that everyone has a chance to share at every meeting or the group will begin to feel like a burden rather than a bonus.
3. How much confidentiality do you want? Are you allowed to discuss the meetings with others? Can you mention names? Should everything be kept at the meetings and go no further, or can general concepts be discussed with family members, friends, and other teachers? I recommend strong confidentiality to build trust. If everyone knows what is said in the group goes no farther, then the likelihood of embarrassment is decreased.
4. There should be a general standing rule that no one offers advice unless asked for advice. You might want to commit the group to silence (attentive listening) while one person talks, unless that person asks a question of the group. I speak from personal experience when I say some of us have thinking styles that absolutely require we put in our "two cents." We need a rule to short-circuit our tendency to interrupt. True listening is a difficult skill to master and absolutely essential to a successful support group. It is best if partners or a group get started on the right foot by making "listening" a rule.
5. Review any rules you have agreed to before every meeting. Choosing a group facilitator may make it easier to keep track of the agreed-upon rules. You can select a facilitator for the next meeting at the end of each session.

▶ *Exercise 6:*
Self-Discovery Activities

The second to fourth times you meet, members share any revelations experienced when doing the activities in chapters 3 through 6. Share personal discoveries about yourself.

> *Share your discoveries. Let your partners share their revelations.*

Perhaps you realize you seldom do any of the things you love most, or you discover there is some interest you have never pursued. Perhaps you have been overlooking and even disregarding some important aspect of your teaching style. Share your discoveries. Let your partners share their revelations.

The idea is to develop trust and rapport within your group. The group should offer acceptance and a forum where you can express even uncomfortable or anxious thoughts. Your partners should feel like peer partners, not advisors or authorities.

Some Final Words

Enjoy and use these tools. Even if you are sporadic about following through with the display space, notebook, and support group, you will still benefit by using them. Do not let your fear of imperfection hold you back from trying. These practices will help you to progress further and faster on this journey. In fact, more often than not these tools will be the energy that powers your journey. For some, using a display space, a notebook, and a support group feels like more work in an already overburdened schedule. You can go through this book without these tools, but you will gain more from everything in this book if you use them.

Early Morning Sorting

Early morning sorting out
before the rush
apricots from a neighbor's
tree, spoiling
on the kitchen counter
The breeze lifting
the curtains, the steam
rising from my second
cup of coffee
The house so fast asleep
I can hear myself think.

—Kathleen Gumm

2

The Heart of a Teacher

*G*ood teaching is not just a matter of being efficient, developing competence, mastering technique and possessing the right kind of knowledge. Good teaching also involves emotional work. It is infused with pleasure, passion, creativity, challenge and joy. It is in Freud's terms, a passionate vocation.

—Andy Hargreaves

Why Pay Attention to Your Heart?

An older school friend teases and then ignores my little girl. Juliet says to me, "It hurts here," pointing to her heart. And I know exactly what she means. Our hearts may be the biological key to maintaining life within our bodies, but our hearts are also something more. It may be the brain that sends those chemical messages that cause our hearts to pound, or shake or give us that shivery, emotional feeling, but as human beings we look to our hearts for the real evaluation of how we are doing. We say things like, "My heart stopped" and "I felt that pounding in my chest." We use our hearts to signify life's deepest emotions: "He broke my heart" and "It filled my heart." And when we feel elated, our hearts reward us by "skipping a beat."

This chapter is devoted to your heart because your emotional center is crucial to your fulfillment as a teacher. Yes, we already discussed the fact that it is possible to go through your career as a teacher in a humdrum manner and survive. But this book is about *thriving*; it is about *loving your work*. And we all know the starting place for any love-related work is the heart.

A teacher's heart is a complex matter. There is the passion that brought you to teaching and the feelings associated with teaching. There is also the spirit within, that part of you that ignites the strength and energy to keep going through the tough times. And that same energy makes you playful and spontaneous within your role as a teacher.

> **Let your students know you value your feelings.**

Within your heart lies the key to continuous interest and excitement about teaching, both the means to avoid burnout and the action that makes your teaching worthwhile. Ignoring the importance and complexity of your feelings is likely to slowly infect your passion for teaching. Your students will know that you have removed emotions from the equation, and if you are devoid of emotion, they can only assume that learning is dull.

Emotions are key to value, including the value of learning. People who have had damage to the emotional areas in their brains cannot feel the difference in value between one choice and another. Their beliefs and motivations become blank. Their minds struggle to accomplish even the most menial tasks because they cannot place an emotional value on even the simplest of decisions. Don't let this be how you teach! Let your students know you value your feelings. Pay attention to your heart, and your attention will reward both you and your students.

As I noted in the discussion on the nature of flow, it is essential that you pay close attention to your inner voice and passions. When a person closes off those messages from within, she stifles the elements that lead to happiness and fulfillment. Use this chapter to devote "attention" to your style, your driving passions, and your spirit. The exercises are designed to accomplish three things:

> *recognition of your unique nature*
> *discovery of your driving passions*
> *knowledge of what brings you joy*

The exercises will help you get a handle on just what makes you tick. They are designed to help uncover the emotional triggers that bring you joy and give you energy. Sounds easy, really. Aren't we all already aware of our own wants and needs?

The truth is that we all have some hidden messages clouding who we are and what we want. Sometimes we need an extra push to see deeper into the pool, past the expectations of our parents and friends and through the labels we received during our growing years. Each exercise will expect you to pay close attention to your subconscious mind. As you respond, listen intently to your mind's voice.

Most of us find our brains can be thinking in many directions at once. Try to accommodate as many of the directions as you can. Put everything down or say it aloud without judgment or critique. That which seems like a silly digression may be the eye-opening self-realization that leads to great personal or professional growth. Be open to the message.

If any particular exercise makes your mind go blank, then skip that exercise. You can always come back later to find you are ready to leap that fence anew. Or perhaps that exercise is just not built for you. No problem; there are plenty more to try. Above all, relax and enjoy the exercises. They are meant to be fun and to offer insight.

By focusing inward, you will take an important first step toward teaching satisfaction and fulfillment. Give up control and allow for stream-of-consciousness thought. Take the time to actually write down your thoughts, or if you have a partner, have a conversation. Use one or all of your "teacher tools" from chapter 1 to respond to these activities. What you do not want to do (if at all possible) is just read and answer the questions in your head. Doing that will limit the amount of fruitful subconscious discovery available in these exercises.

You Are Unique!

Tap into your unique style as a teacher. No two people are exactly alike and knowing how you are different as a teacher will help you recognize and fully use your special skills in the job.

Two of my high school teachers were tremendously successful and entirely different: Dr. Smull taught biology. He was a humorist, starting each class with a gross joke, occasionally letting snakes out of their cages to hear the screams of students, and making timed tests a cacophony of screams and flying papers by slamming a ruler down as each minute passed. He made us all laugh. He made biology fun and we learned anyway. Even struggling students opted to take his difficult courses because they knew the classes would never be dull. When you finished one semester you knew a great deal of biology and a number of good jokes as well.

In contrast, Ms. Baumgarten was the queen of structure and organization. Her English and college prep classes required students to keep detailed notes about the requirements of each assignment and to begin immediately in silent journals once you entered the classroom. Her lecture style was serious and her assignments were intense. If you didn't get started on the first step on the correct date, you would already be too far behind to sufficiently catch up. The discipline and high expectations prepared students well for the rigors of college, and any students I talked with commented on how glad they were that they took Ms. Baumgarten in preparation for college essay exams.

I believe Ms. Baumgarten found as much joy in her way of teaching as Dr. Smull found in his. She smiled often and seldom missed a day of teaching, not the signs of an unhappy teacher.

Granted, their styles were completely different, but their success was apparent in the success of their students. And they managed to enjoy their work in their own unique ways.

Doing what we do best means first recognizing the ways in which we are special. Teaching is a complex exercise filled with many opportunities for various abilities and interests to shine through. The first set of activities in this chapter is meant to help you recognize your unique teaching qualities.

▶ *Exercise 1:*
What Kind of Teacher Are You?

Take a few minutes to describe yourself as a teacher. Give us an overview that describes yourself and your work. Don't take long to think about it; just write the first five to ten teaching characteristics that come to mind. Start with "I teach . . . "

Now read your response. Did you say something like "I teach third grade at Mitchell Elementary in San Fernando. I teach cursive writing, multiplication and division, health and getting to know the neighborhood. I like teaching because I like to work with kids. I'm best at reading, not crazy about math"? Or did you say something like "I teach high school. I teach using slide and lecture format. My students are required to do projects and a final exam. I teach physics and chemistry, and I'm occasionally asked to cover health. I'm a tough teacher. I

Part 1: Know Yourself

don't extend deadlines or accept below par work. I demand the most from my students and I'm known throughout campus as a tough grader"?

Try the same exercise in a slightly different way to see if we can shed some more light on the here and now of who you are as a teacher. Write a few sentences or short paragraph again, but this time start with "I teach in order to . . . " You will gain much more insight if you let your subconscious mind do the talking on this exercise. Worry about accuracy later. Please allow your subconscious full rein in this exercise. If it tells you to write or say something, write it. Don't stop to think if it is true or false. Don't get into a debate with your subconscious.

> **Who you are brings a great deal extra to the classroom.**

If you are anything like me there will be an interesting difference between the first and second exercise. The first exercise probably elicited information and judgment calls about who you are as a teacher. "I teach math"; "I'm weak at paperwork, but great at explaining"; "I like kids." The second exercise probably dug up some thoughts from the heart, things about your basic nature that made you want to become a teacher. "I teach in order to stand in front of people and perform, I love to captivate an audience"; "I teach in order to give; it fills me up inside. I feel like a saint"; "I teach in order to change the world; it makes me feel powerful. I feel like I make a difference"; "I teach in order to help children."

Probably the second exercise is more revealing about why you ended up teaching. The first passage on the whole would be easy to read to a friend; the second might feel too revealing and a little scary to share. Who am I to think I have this power and ability? Where did I get all these deep-seated needs?

If your answer was something like, "I teach in order to make a living. I need to support my family," or "I teach in order to avoid doing what I'm really meant to do," don't snarl, hate yourself, or plead insanity. This is very good information to know. It is important you map out a path to fulfill your true self. On the way it can't hurt if you happen to be an outstanding teacher. Besides who you are brings a great deal extra to the classroom. And what can be better teaching for students than a person en route to their chosen destination? Modeling such a journey is the best kind of teaching. The exercises in this book can help you bring that real self into the classroom, which will help you feel better about teaching and be a better teacher because of it.

It's important to dig deeper into our subconscious to see what we really think our potential and capabilities as a teacher are. For this I recommend two metaphorical exercises.

▶ *Exercise 2:*
Metaphor 1

Compare your teaching to a color. Start your paragraph with "I teach . . . (blue? green? aqua? chartreuse?)." Take your time picking the color. Look in a box of crayons if you have a box handy. Believe your subconscious mind in this exercise. If you are thinking blue and your inner heart is screaming electric aquamarine, go with the screaming soul of you; it knows something you do not yet recognize. Following is my response to this exercise: "I teach blue-green like a tree growing branches, like a lawn, fresh, clean and green, excited to greet the day, like an ocean, still in the morning, crystal clear, cloudy and foreboding in the afternoon. Sometimes filled with waves, uneven but powerful, sometimes, calm. Always leading my students to realize the excitement of depth and the mystery of learning!"

Revealing? Now you try it; see how many revelations you can elicit from your subconscious mind. Every time you feel blank, just start again with "I teach" and see what pops into your mind. Write whatever it tells you to write down; you can critique the accuracy later.

You can extend this metaphorical exercise by trying a variety of colors to see what projections they elicit. "I teach yellow like . . . "; "I teach red like . . . " Because we don't tend to judge color, comparing our teaching to a color allows us to remove judgment from our aspirations and teaching style. We recognize color as a style or quality. Some of the very traits we might list in color and feel proud about might seem negative if we just added them to a list of teacher traits. For instance, one teacher who tried this exercise said her teaching was red because of her stubborn willfulness and the temperature of her teaching. She felt red gave meaning to her incessant drive and high expectations. She confessed that her passion is good for many students, but sometimes overwhelms others (and administrators!). Describing these traits as a color allowed her to recognize the positive sides of these traits and allowed her to appreciate her special style as a teacher while noting also where she needed to improve.

What did you uncover about yourself? My blue-green response made me realize how much I enjoy the mysteries inherent in learning. I'd spent a great deal of time trying to have all the answers because I thought as a teacher, I should know all the answers. This approach greatly limited my ability to go further and further into each subject area. After this exercise, I realized it was okay to tell students, "I honestly don't know," then to work with them to find answers, which always led to more questions. Together we could uncover the depths of learning, and I did not always have to be an expert; I could be a learner, too.

Part 1: Know Yourself

When you finish this exercise, I hope you will have made some discoveries. I hope when you read your response you will be blushing. If you are, that is good! It is a sign of your pride (and embarrassment) about the greatness within your heart. The intent of the first part of this book is to help you sharpen your understanding of the potentials within.

▶ *Exercise 3:*
Metaphor 2

Again, it is best if you let go of mental reins and allow free-range thoughts. This exercise removes judgment by asking you to compare yourself to an animal. Don't snarl and growl! Let yourself go and you might be surprised at what your response reveals about your inner aspirations. Answer this question: If an animal could teach, what kind of animal-teacher would you be and why?

Did you decide giraffe so you could be really tall and see ahead for miles? Or perhaps you picked Tyrannosaurus Rex because then you could be certain of the rapt attention of your kindergarten class (if not, you could always eat them). Does the animal you selected reveal anything about your temperament, your teaching style, or both? Would your students guess you picked this animal?

Go over your color and animal metaphors, then jot down three reasons why the metaphors fit and three reasons they do not fit. This exercise will give you some insights into the ideal teacher you are in your heart versus the actual teacher you are in the classroom. Plus it gives your thinking self a chance to debate the details with your feeling self—nothing like balancing the yin and the yang.

▶ *Exercise 4:*
Taking a Closer Look

Some features of your teaching style may have come into focus through the metaphorical exercises. Now let's try something opposite to the metaphor. Pay attention to concrete, real-life clues about who you are. Become Sherlock Holmes and take a little walk through the places where you post clues about who you are. Check your classroom and home, your purse or briefcase, your gym locker or desk, and your vehicle.

What clues do you find about who you are? Movie ticket stubs and candy wrappers? Which movies and what kinds of candy? What station is your radio tuned to? What do you hang on your walls and leave on your tables? Are there any patterns? Certain colors or designs? Do you collect anything? What kinds of books do you leave out and which have you actually read? Are you methodically organized or spontaneously haphazard?

Look, touch, and make notes as if you were trying to solve a case by wandering through the belongings of a suspect. What kind of a teacher would you expect to come from these environments? Make guesses as to the teacher's temperament: Loud or quiet? Ordered or wild? Cautious or bold? What are the teacher's favorite pastimes? Colors? Music? What is this teacher likely to get out of teaching? How does this teacher probably behave in class? If possible, take a friend with you on this exploration to keep you from making rash judgments that are not based on the clues at hand.

▶ *Exercise 5:*
Standing in Line
When you are in line at the grocery store, where does your mind go? Do you daydream, calculate your checkbook, or read the headlines from the magazine rack? When you read the headlines, which ones catch your eye? What articles intrigue you and which ones do you skim right over?

Taken together these self-reflective exercises should give you some overall ideas about your teaching style. You will find your style probably coincides quite a bit with the way you are as a person. If we all try to be carbon copies of one another, we lose the energy and emotion that is present in our individual teaching styles. Above all I advocate recognizing and tapping into your unique qualities.

Are some teaching styles better than other styles? I imagine that depends on the student, and the circumstance and the development of the teacher. A teacher who has paid attention to his style and honed it will probably find it to be an asset rather than a nuisance. A teacher who does not recognize and appreciate her teaching style may suffocate her natural ways to try to be more like other teachers. That battle against her style will damage her attempts to be her best.

One aim of this book is to help you see and appreciate the positive characteristics embedded in your natural teaching style. So, you are a quiet, shy teacher who prefers small groups to front-of-the-room, explosive lectures? Terrific! Recognize and develop that specialty. The value of small-group, cooperative student interaction is becoming more and more recognized in educational circles. So, you are a raging maniac who has an opinion about everything and is absolutely on fire in front of your students? Excellent! Your students know you really love the subject matter. Incorporate debate and speech-making skills into your instruction. Your students will have the benefit of you as a role model.

Too often we teachers attempt to be just like the teachers we admire without considering our own special gifts. Students are all different; so are teachers. If we buy into the idea that each of our students is a unique learner, then we must also recognize that each of us is a unique teacher. As my eldest child has gone through school, she hasn't had the same kind of teacher twice. It has afforded her the opportunity of varied learning experiences. Some of her teachers have been better matched to her needs than others. That does not discount their valuable teaching. They probably were well-suited to the needs of a different group of students. This diversity does not, of course, excuse us from reaching out and learning more ways of teaching. It only serves to help us support and defend our natural gifts.

Finding Your Driving Passions

We are special as teachers. We bring our own set of skills and interests to the job. We also have one main drive that arouses our passions as teachers, and probably as people. Your passion might have nudged forth when you finished the sentence "I teach in order to . . . " Did you find yourself ranting on about the importance of guiding young people? Voila! You have probably tapped into your guiding passion. Csikzentmihalyi says the key to a lifetime of happiness lies in the ability to find a worthwhile guiding purpose for your life challenges and goals. So many activities inherent in the act of teaching give us the opportunity to pursue a guiding life purpose. Yet another reason teaching is an ideal career choice.

I met a school counselor who claimed her lifetime goal to be the eradication of gangs in Los Angeles. Wow! I figure that certainly is enough of a job to keep her busy for a lifetime. And her chosen purpose has very clear feedback. Each gang member she converts, each gang she closes down, each time gang membership drops, she can feel good about her participation and dedication. She said she formulated that goal because she believes a solid, worthwhile goal is essential to self-esteem and achievement. Csikzentmihalyi would agree and probably applaud.

If you already have a clear model of your driving passion as a teacher then you are one step ahead, but you may want to do these exercises anyway. Sometimes well-meaning people lead us astray from our own true motivations. They say, "No, you are meant for this or that," and we believe them. Or perhaps we changed directions because we thought we had too many limitations to pursue what really turned us on. Use these exercises to identify the most motivating, exciting thing about teaching for you.

Exercise 6:
▶ **A Great Day in the Classroom**

We all have good teaching days and bad teaching days. This exercise is about remembering or imagining a great teacher day. You walk out of school on cloud nine because . . . because what? What three things can happen in your classroom that fill you up, make you dance on air, give you energy for the rest of the day, or month, or year? Remember a time such a day happened first. Then, if nothing comes to you from your memory scrapbook, imagine a day in which you walk out of school feeling proud, fulfilled, excited, energized. The key here is to answer the question, what happened? What three things sent you over the top? Can you imagine three things that would make this day a reality for you? (One small rule: the three things must relate to teaching, not winning the lottery.)

Examine your perfect day closely to find clues about your driving passion. When you imagined your great day, were you excited by the enthusiasm of your students? Did that cause your heart to beat faster? If you were jazzed because they became excited as a group, your driving passion could be a number of things. It could be the pleasure you gain from sharing your love of the subject matter. It could be the attention you garner from your student cheering section. It could even be the way they launched into their own individual understandings of the subject matter.

> *The key to finding the authentic you . . . is to feel it in your heart.*

Understand that the key to finding the authentic you, the passions that drive you as a teacher, is to feel it in your heart. That chemical burning sensation that makes you think your heart is bursting through your chest is the one that says, "Here, this is why you teach." It may even feel close to the sensation of fear. It ought to make you afraid; it is vitally important to your teaching success.

How do you get closer to the "heart" of what excited you? Try separating your feelings. If you think it was the attention that you were enjoying, imagine getting the same attention from a string of jokes and stories rather than the lesson. If that feels satisfying, then you are right; it was the attention that made your day! If that is not satisfying, imagine the same day and lessons occurring, but you are not actually in front of the room teaching. This time you are in the wings, and a student teacher is giving the lesson you prepared. It is still your material and you are sharing it with your students, but you are not the deliverer. Does that hold the same level of excitement or did you wish you were up front delivering the material? What about if your students learned the material at home and came in excited to share with you all of their wonderful new discoveries? Are you as jazzed as if you taught them yourself? Most of us would have some combination of feelings for each of these scenarios, but try to tap into the one that holds the strongest feelings for you; it may be the main thing that drives your teaching.

▶ *Exercise 7:*
Reverse That

Now imagine a miserable day of teaching. What three things can happen that bury you, sap your energy, make you want to give up and escape? Were you unable to help a student who needed you? Did your students act bored and disinterested? Was your lesson and material rote or disorganized? Sometimes the thing that does not happen is the thing you need most to tap into your driving passion.

These exercises might not directly point you to your "big purpose." You may have to play detective to uncover the big idea inherent in small, day-to-day successes or failures.

▶ *Exercise 8:*
Lost in the Moment

Think of a teaching time when you became lost in the moment. If it happened more than once, what did the experiences have in common? Were you driven by internal forces? Highly motivated? Remember details. Can you tap into where your drive was coming from? What was happening? What were you doing and what were your students doing? Was it a planned moment or an accident?

▶ *Exercise 9:*
Teacher Movies

Have you seen *Stand and Deliver, Dead Poet's Society,* or *Dangerous Minds*? A host of teacher movies exist, and now you can even catch the American Teacher Awards on television. Watch these programs alone or with your support group and see if any inner fires are lit. If during any of these programs you feel a welling up of pride or an excitement about teaching, you may be tapping into your driving motivation for teaching. Can you put it into specific words? Pictures?

If you feel like you have not yet nailed the key to your driving passion, you may uncover more in chapter 4, "The Soul of a Teacher." Often, I find the heart and soul are quite intertwined when it comes to identifying a lifetime purpose.

The Joy of Teaching and Other Things

And finally we need to discuss joy. Different people experience and feel joy differently, but as a teacher you need to take your joy into account. The playful, happy part of you needs to be nurtured and protected. I think this nurturance is necessary for all people, but it is especially true for teachers. Our job is to help others. Anybody in a helping profession is in danger of being drained. It is an overused cliché, but true nonetheless: if your cup is empty you will no longer be able to fill the cups of the people who need you. If you don't keep your joy alive, its lack will infect your teaching and the ability of your students to learn from you.

▶ *Exercise 10:*
Find Your Joy

Forget about teaching in this exercise; concentrate on your whole person and the things that make you happy. List all the things you love to do or think you would love to do. When you stop, find yourself at a dead-end after only three ideas, take a deep breath and list silly things until you come up with more ideas. List more than twenty-five viable ideas before you quit. You must keep going because there may be things you have forgotten out of neglect. Joy is something that slowly dissipates when you pay no attention. You need at least twenty-five to be sure you are not forgetting some quiet part of yourself. Think about music, art, dance, physical activity, food, entertainment, and your social life. Think about the activities you used to do before you got busy, older, or less active. Write it all down because the next exercise asks you about items on this list.

▶ *Exercise 11:*
Checks and Stars

1. Put a check mark next to every activity on your list that you have done within the last three months. If you make fewer than three check marks you are in serious joy neglect.
2. Put stars next to each activity that you really love to do or are excited about trying out. If you have fewer than three stars you may need to get to know yourself a little better.
3. Underline any activity you can do cheaply (for less than ten dollars) and easily. If you have fewer than three items underlined, you may need to do some additional brainstorming.
4. Circle three things that you also enjoyed as a child. If no such activities exist on your list, think back on your childhood and find at least three previously adored activities.

Finding the things that bring you joy is essential to your fulfillment. You might be wondering what all these ideas have to do with your teaching. Plenty. If you are fulfilling your need for play and joy, you are much more likely to have that energy and attitude affect your teaching. If you are not playing enough, it is very possible low energy and a tired attitude are affecting your teaching. In addition, if you tap into the playful part of yourself, you may find ways to incorporate those joys into your teaching.

I know a teacher who is also a musician and all of her bulletin boards have a musical theme. She plays classical CDs during school transitions. There was a story a few years back about a runner/teacher who attracted all of his elementary students to join him in a jog three days a week before school. Seems not only did they have fun together, the students were also more alert and ready to learn when the morning bell rang. What special joy can you incorporate into your classroom?

Additional Brainstorming

You know the lottery dream we all love to create in our minds? The one where you hit the big one and you throw a big secret party for everyone you love? Doesn't that fantasy alone make the $1.00 purchase price a worthy expenditure?

To fully capture your sources of joy I want you to experience that fantasy in a number of different ways. First, enjoy it in its original form. You have won enough money, freedom, and time to make your life anything you desire. What do you wish for? Write down or share your ideas with your support group. You may enjoy creating a collage of your fantasy on your display space: Things you wish to buy, places you want to visit, and so on. Revel in it. The following rules apply, however, to this and the following fantasies:

- You may not spend your time or money on debts, errands, or duties.
- You must create at least ten scenarios.
- You must exclude television, movies, and the newspaper from your possibilities.

Try a similar fantasy, but this time you have been handed one month and $50,000 that you may not spend on prior debts. Now what do you wish for and how do you spend your time? Again, think about looking through the travel section of your newspaper, or cut out pictures from catalogs and magazines. Enjoy your thoughts as if they were special little gifts for the mind. Now imagine you get only one day and $100, then less than an hour and only $10 (this is the teacher version of this fantasy).

One person fantasized a quiet space in a park and having white paper and a box of colored markers. Another bought a classical CD and took his headphones out on a local nature trail. A third played chess with her daughter and another collected dried leaves for displays. Your ideas will be your own, but listen closely to what they tell you.

▶ *Exercise 12:*
Other Joys

If you were not a teacher, what would you be? Think of at least five other occupations that interest you. You do not need training or expertise, just an interest, desire to learn, or curiosity. Remember, this is a fantasy. Do not worry about your perceived limitations.

> **Don't neglect the simple joys you can create now.**

Your alternative occupations may be far from teaching. They may even be opposite in scope and skill. They may reveal some part of your nature that you should explore. Are your other careers less intense or more adventurous? Do they lean toward some talent such as acting or painting? Is it possible to nurture these aspirations in other ways, inside or outside of the classroom? Think about it.

Taken together, these exercises point to a very important activity that you must engage in regularly: nurturing your inner self. Ignoring your happiness will have dire consequences on your mental and emotional health.

Have you played lately? You might cringe and say, "Who has the time?" My guess is you have found the time to read or listen to the news, an activity that can have a horrible effect on your emotional well-being. And you probably have watched at least a show or two on TV this week, another activity that is vegetatively nice, but that does nothing for your heart and soul. Spend thought and energy finding ways to incorporate your wishes and needs into your life. Winning the lottery would be really nice, but don't neglect the simple joys you can create now. You need it. We all do.

Chapter Assignments

Okay. You have engaged in a series of activities designed to open your eyes to who you are as a teacher and where your heart is as a teacher. I hope that, by going through these exercises, you have uncovered or rediscovered a few things:

- What motivates and excites you?
- What is your driving passion as a teacher?
- What frustrates you?
- What qualities are part of your teaching style?
- What do you bring to the table?
- What is missing from the table?
- What three strengths do you see in yourself?
- What quality, skill, or knowledge do you wish you had?
- What are your special life joys, small things that bring you happiness?

Now what to do with all this knowledge?
1. Put all your thoughts and ideas someplace where they will not get lost. You can file them, post them, or trust a friend to nag and remind you, but do not lose your thoughts and ideas.
2. Begin to do things that bring you joy, regularly. Take time at least once a week for special, uplifting activities. Keep your list handy if you are likely to forget. Teachers can be martyrs; it comes with the job. This assignment is to ignore your problems and pressures at least one hour once a week for the benefit of your heart. (It also benefits those around you because they appreciate your improved mood.)
3. Think of one or two ways to incorporate "play" into your teaching day.
4. Value, appreciate, and express your emotions in the classroom. Students need to know that you care, that you have emotions about teaching and about learning.

On a Slow Hour

Under the leaf green shade
where the creek ended
I sat with uncertainty.
The leaves made me a tent
It was damp and quiet there

and I was still
in the slow of that hour

Until all of the sky gathered
into an orange and black
winged shower falling
down, all around
my green bank of reasoning

The lady bugs were hatching
I made one thousand wishes.

—Kathleen Gumm

3

The Mind of a Teacher

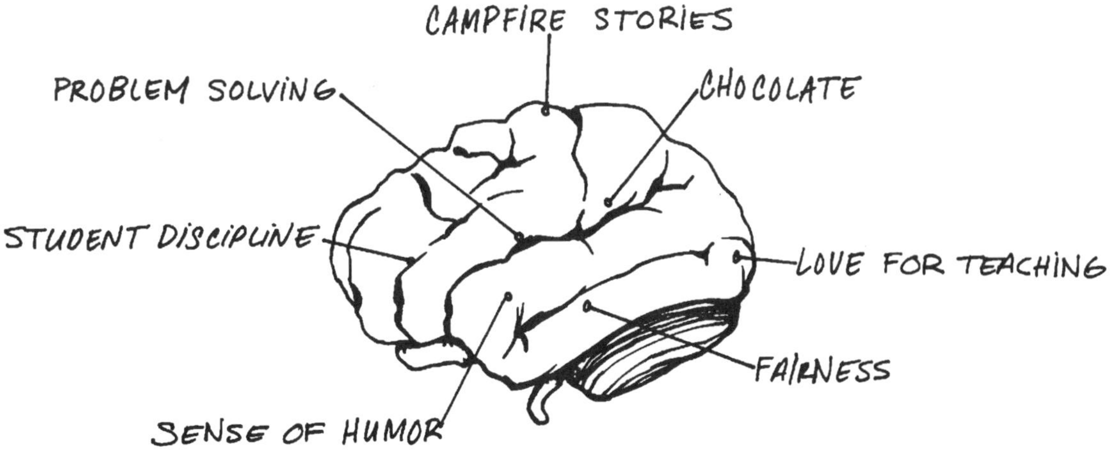
CAMPFIRE STORIES
PROBLEM SOLVING
CHOCOLATE
STUDENT DISCIPLINE
LOVE FOR TEACHING
FAIRNESS
SENSE OF HUMOR

How many educators who enjoin their students to be good readers haven't themselves enjoyed reading a book for pleasure in years? How many teachers ask students to be high achievers in math and science but themselves lack any enthusiasm for the great discoveries being made in those fields or no longer ask the basic wide-eyed questions about the universe or about the origins of life that have inspired the greatest scientists of every age?

—Thomas Armstrong

Part 1: Know Yourself

A teacher was in the grocery store shopping when an ex-student dragged his mother over to visit. "Hi, Ms. Smith. Would you show my mom your journal? She doesn't believe me." Ms. Smith laughed and dragged out the journal with its torn edges and worn cover. The mother smiled at her son and said, "Okay, okay, I believe it." This was not the first time students asked to see Ms. Smith's journal, but this time she realized the significance of their requests. The students loved seeing proof that their teacher, too, was learning and growing.

Athletes work out to stay in shape and to surpass what they have previously accomplished. Teachers study. We have a lot to keep up on. A teacher's mind is a critical part of the teacher toolbox.

Teaching is complex and it requires you to develop your mind on many levels. Yes, we need to know about the subject we are teaching, but we also need to know about our students. How do they learn? What motivates them? We need to know about curriculum requirements and instructional strategies, but we also need to know about ourselves. When am I at my best as a teacher? What teaching tools do I need to develop? How can I best keep my temperament in check? My thinking sharp? Staying ahead of educational trends means knowing about the brain and educational research as well as about political fluctuations and local opinion. The truth is, becoming a teacher means never running out of material to learn! Your mind is your vehicle to successful teaching.

Don't let the requirements overwhelm you! Think of teaching as a chance to grow. Your students will respect and learn from you if they see you take on the learning challenges posed by teaching rather than hiding behind rote methods and canned answers. The best teaching advice a mentor ever spoke was, "Respond to questions with a question and never be afraid to say, 'Gosh! I don't know. Where might we find that out?'" It is not a teaching requirement to be brilliant and perfect, but it is our job to be experts at learning and finding the answers.

This chapter is about finding out what you need to know in order to teach well. Knowledge is a key ingredient to successful teaching and a complex realm of professional development. So where should you start? What are the areas of knowledge that we need to address as teachers? What are all the areas of mind development required of teachers? How do you decide which to pursue first?

Teacher Knowledge

Knowing your subject does not guarantee your teaching will be exceptional. How many of us can remember a college science professor or high school social studies teacher who was a proficient scientist or historian, but unable to share that skill and knowledge with others? Knowledge of teaching methodology helps, but then there still may be a gap between the methods and the students. Knowledge of students, their learning differences and personal histories, may allow for better communication of the subject matter, but what if you are less than well informed about the subject you are teaching? The latitude of learning required to teach is immense.

> **Becoming a teacher means never running out of material to learn!**

You do not have to know everything right now in order to teach. Start with areas of weakness and keep growing. Each new piece of learning you master will mean more success and excitement. I especially recommend knowing where you can seek out more knowledge and information. The resource list may give you some ideas where to begin some of your searches.

Knowing Yourself

Teachers are often expected to know about everything under the sun, but only recently has the discussion of self-reflection come to the forefront. Self-reflection will help you understand your own strengths and weaknesses, your needs and wants as a teacher, and your higher motivations.

For your growth I recommend that you spend some time with the reflection exercises in this book and that you seriously commit your time to a support group and journal writing. Beyond this book you may want to look at the ideas Caine, Caine, and Crowell (1994) explore in *MindShifts,* as well those Goleman (1995) explores in *Emotional Intelligence.* Those resources will give you a large lead in the area of self-reflection and self-knowledge.

Knowing Your Subject Matter

Clearly, if you are teaching a subject then it is expected that you will have some measure of mastery of the skills and information pertaining to that subject. But how do you determine what skills and data are important to know? What resources can you go to for more information, knowledge, and skill development? How is this subject best learned?

I recommend two methods to ensure the information you teach is important, accurate, and relevant to your students: Become an expert, and become a learner. An expert is extremely well versed and capable within a field. If you are teaching history, well versed does not mean you spout off historic facts as though you were trying to get on "Jeopardy." It is fun to know lots of facts, but such knowledge will not necessarily translate into your students' understanding the importance of information. No, to be an expert means you act as a historian acts. For instance, you may have already formulated your family's genealogy and joined the local historical society. You give tours of the local historical buildings and document old photographs for the library.

> **Your students will know the material is relevant because you behave as if it is relevant.**

Do you need to go this far if you are simply teaching the fourth-grade "Know your local community" curriculum? No, but it will certainly convince your students that you believe what they are learning is important and relevant. You will have a deep personal understanding to communicate to your students. The importance of what you are teaching will shine through in the commitment you have already made to the subject matter. Everything you do as a genealogist and a local historian will become part of what you "sell" as you teach about local history. Your students will know the material is relevant because you behave as if it is relevant.

Suppose, for example, that you are asked to teach algebra and you were never a big fan of math. Where do you begin? If you decide to become an expert, then the place to start is at your local college or adult school. Take algebra, algebra II, calculus, as many courses as you need to take to become proficient and confident with numbers and equations. Be sure to learn what all the skills are good for: How are these subjects used by real people in work situations? Join an association of math teachers, or better yet, mathematicians. Once you have reached a reasonable level of mastery, teaching the subject will be easy, but more importantly, your students will see that you have invested your energy so it must have value.

What if you teach too many subjects to become well versed in them all? Or what if the particular subject area is just not one that sparks your interest? Your other option is simple. Become a learning partner with your students. Develop your interest and your knowledge and bring your students along. Search for the relevance as you present and learn the material. Yes, the text and curriculum materials will be your guide, but to those you add the natural questions of an inquisitive and interested mind. You and your students ask questions and pursue strains of information within the subject matter. Perhaps the first and foremost questions need to be "Why do people study this? What makes this subject worthwhile and meaningful to learn?" When the questions and the avenues you pursue are not automatically available within the curriculum materials you have been provided, side-by-side with your students you seek out places and people who can answer your questions. You become a bit of a detective because you want to find out, and your students are learning with you about how much more there is beyond the scope of textbook coverage. You are doing what is called *seeking depth*, and it is the key to overcoming those age-old student questions: "Why are we learning this? What does it matter?" If you, as their teacher, can answer that question with confidence, the chances of motivating your students to learn the subject matter are high!

In this case, if you were asked to teach math, you might realize that you will never go so far as to take upper level math courses and join math associations. You can choose to become a learner with your students. Yes, you will need to have basic skills to teach them the skills they need, but be open and go beyond the lessons in the book. Look at each unit and ask, "Why learn this? Who uses this information and skill?" Ask questions with your students: How come? Why? When? What if . . . ? Imagine a great mystery behind the numbers. Imagine the numbers and letters are trying to teach you a great lesson about life. Apply the math equations to something that interests you: sports, art, music, education. If you do not have an automatic love of equations, then perhaps you can at least develop a sincere appreciation for their worth. Find out why it is part of the curriculum, and adopt it as something worthwhile to learn. If you learn more and decide it is not a useful skill or knowledge for your students, then perhaps you need to become an educational leader (see more in chapter 15) and begin to communicate to others why this material should not be part of the curriculum.

> *Ask questions with your students.*

These two approaches work in "nonacademic" areas, as well. Suppose you are asked to teach soccer and you have never participated in the sport. You can get out a book on soccer and learn the basic rules and plays, but probably neither you nor your students are going to be particularly motivated to learn the game. So you end up kicking the ball around the field a bit and giving a multiple choice test on the rules of and plays in soccer. The students are happy to move on to the next sport; perhaps it will be more interesting.

Now imagine that, instead, you decide to become a colearner with your students. You go to a local game. You bring in a local star to talk about the sport. You take a coach's clinic to learn how to teach the basic skills. You bring back and share with your students all that you are learning and ask them to seek out soccer lovers to learn more. Your enthusiasm and knowledge climbs together. If they know you have decided to join an adult league, their motivation to learn the sport will catapult.

Part 1: Know Yourself

▶ *Exercise 1:*
Value of My Subject

Write down your subject and a list of the basic subdivisions of your subject, things you will cover throughout the year or unit. Next to each item on your list, answer these questions and others that you think will help you learn the importance of your subject:

- Who needs this information and why?
- When is it used?
- How well does a person need to know how to do this?

For example, all people use decimals in money transactions, and scientists and engineers use them to calculate to exact amounts. Cooks use fractions to measure ingredients and others use them to refer to parts of things. Learning about the original colonies of the United States helps people to understand the social and cultural foundations that started our nation; if we understand our beginnings we have a clearer picture of the many early influences over our laws and culture today.

If you struggle and do not have adequate answers, then begin your research. Find someone who values this material and ask her why it is valuable. Seek out an expert who can demonstrate how this material is used in the real world. If it is simply a building-block skill, something that leads to more important skills, know this. Share what you have learned with your students or ask your students to find out what is important about learning this material.

Knowing Your Students

How well you can know your students is going to vary from teaching situation to teaching situation. A university professor teaching large seminars with one hundred or more students is unlikely to get a clear picture of each and every student, and it is probably not necessary to do so. The professor should have some idea about the variety of students in his classroom, what kinds of backgrounds they come from, why they are taking the course, and what prior knowledge they might bring to the learning.

On the other hand, an elementary teacher needs a greater knowledge of his students. Who are they? How do they learn best? What influences may affect their learning? What is the cultural and ethnic diversity here?

Teachers can gain knowledge about their students in a number of ways. Use the first few weeks of school to become familiar with your students. Look through their school records. Observe them during recess and passing periods. Watch them in their groups and when they are working independently. Some teachers schedule interview time with each student and take notes as to their interests, successes, thoughts on school and learning. Or consider designing a survey for students that you can use to gain insight into their interests and concerns. One very effective method many teachers use is the exchange journal. The exchange journal goes back and forth from student to teacher like an ongoing conversation. The teacher does not always need to comment on the student entries. Many teachers rotate their journal interaction from student group to student group, so it does not become overwhelming to respond.

> *Gain some insight into the student's attitudes and feelings about school.*

When I was in a teacher training program, a very wise mentor suggested calling every parent before the first month of school had finished. Report something interesting about the class or student to the parents and try to gain some insight into the student's attitudes and feelings about school. The mentor suggested this exercise as a way to touch base with parents on a positive note, so that if the time came to call about a discipline or learning concern, you had established rapport. I see it as yet another opportunity for knowing your students better. If you make these calls, be sure to have an idea what you will ask or tell the parents before you pick up the phone. I usually ask if they have noted any particular strengths in their child so that I might take note of them during the school year.

Look for other teachers that have good rapport with students and ask them how they develop their relationships. There is always a wealth of information sitting in your staff room.

▶ *Exercise 2:*
Value of My Students

List five to ten short questions to ask your students that will help you understand something about them beyond the classroom and the grades they make.

Knowing Teaching Techniques and Strategies

Do you know the best way to present a lesson? Are you aware of effective teaching strategies? Most teachers have had numerous staff development seminars and workshops on teaching techniques and strategies. In addition, textbook companies often include many strategies as part of the teacher's preparation materials.

Part 1: Know Yourself

Nevertheless, we all know there is always more to learn. Teaching is both an art and a science, which means one lesson presentation is never enough to meet all the needs in your classroom, or your needs as a teacher.

Discover new methods of teaching by remaining open when you hear about new techniques and strategies. Read publications that will constantly introduce you to new teaching ideas and join an educational organization that will give you opportunities to attend workshops and learn new methods. Talk to other teachers at your site or at other sites. Find out what they are trying out in their classrooms and consider observing other teachers while they teach. Attend a workshop, ask a teacher who uses the technique, try it out in your classroom. Some techniques may never suit your teaching approach, but do not negate everything about the method. You may discover some portion of what you have learned is entirely applicable. Most experienced teachers have a battery of strategies and resources at their fingertips and are always open and looking for new ways to present learning.

▶ *Exercise 3:*
Value of Techniques and Strategies

Choose one lesson that you have used before. Ask a fellow teacher if he or she can think of another way to teach that particular learning objective. Use and evaluate the second method. Is it worth adding to your repertoire?

Knowing Educational Research and Trends

What is the latest information on learning and teaching? How much of the research has been verified in the classroom? Do you realize how much is being revealed about learning through recent brain research? The field of neuroscience is exploding with new information about how the brain processes information, and much of it is being tested successfully in classrooms. Are you aware of such educational terminology as Accelerated Learning, multiple intelligence theory, learning styles, brain-based learning, and parallel processing? If these words sound familiar you are on track with recent research. If you are unsure about what all these mean and how they apply to the classroom, it may be time to begin your foray into brain research. Try reading material by Robert Sylwester, Renate and Geoffrey Caine, or Howard Gardner. Some of their material is in the reference list. Attend workshops or form a reading club.

Brain research is nothing to be frightened of; it has very exciting implications for educators. The best news of all is that much of what you discover matches much of what we already do in the classroom!

Knowing Resources

Where can you get the best information? Who can help you when you don't know how to do something or where to find something? Obviously, if I recommend you go beyond the textbooks when teaching a subject, then it becomes imperative that you know how to find more information. As I said earlier, if you choose not to become an expert, then you must become a real learner, someone who is exploring the subject with students.

If you begin to ponder questions outside of the curriculum materials, then you need also to know where to go looking for the answers.

- Rule 1: Befriend a Librarian. These folks are an amazing help. The more connected they are to a large-scale public library or a university library, the more they will be able to point the way to more and better resources.
- Rule 2: Announce What You Are Seeking. Put up a notice in your staff room, ask your students to ask at home, tell everyone you know that you are seeking this person, item, or bit of information.

Knowing Technology

Gardner (1991) shows a strong link between intelligence and technology. This link is so strong we cannot actually separate intelligence from the use of technology. Obviously if Galileo were alive today, he could not produce discoveries of the magnitude and importance of his earlier observations unless he learned to work with the technology of today. We cannot separate what our students need to learn and know from the tools they must use to make their learning happen. So ask yourself, "How are my students going to be expected to apply technology in their lives? What skills do they need to know to succeed?"

These skills are not fluff. They are essential to success. When I took college chemistry I was flabbergasted at the speed and agility with which the younger students used the calculator. I had to quickly catch up on calculator skills in order to survive because the problems were miles beyond the solve-in-your-head technique! Does anyone doubt that the students we teach today are going to rely on computer and satellite technology beyond anything we can presently imagine? Do not leave them behind because of your own fear of technology. Take every course offered. Get a home computer as soon as you can muster the funds. Become a technology-proficient teacher and apply it in your classroom.

The chart on page 36 will help you organize your thoughts concerning all these areas of knowledge. Instead of letting it overwhelm you, set and meet small goals in each area. Recognize there will always be more to learn and enjoy the process of learning.

Table 1: Knowledge Development

Area to Develop	What to Know	Potential Tools	One Goal
Knowledge of Self	Interests, drives, passions, hot buttons, energy boosters and sappers, strengths, weaknesses	Journal, teacher reflection or support group, reflection partner	
Knowledge of Subject Matter	Who uses this subject? When? How? Why? What is important for my students to know, understand, and be able to do?	Become an expert, join associations, take higher-level courses, read, become an explorer, ask questions, seek answers.	
Knowledge of Students	How do they learn? What are their strengths and weaknesses? What are their interests and cultural backgrounds?	Student and parent surveys, phone call surveys, read up on cultural and ethnic background, diagnose learning styles	
Knowledge of Techniques and Strategies	What are some standard and alternative methods for presenting lessons? How can I vary my lessons to meet the variety of student needs?	Observe and question other teachers, join associations, read teacher publications, take workshops.	
Knowledge of Research and Trends	What does research tell us about learning and teaching that can help me reach my students more effectively?	Join research associations, read research articles, take a workshop on brain research, learning research, or educational research.	
Knowledge of Resources	Where can I get tools and resources I need to teach my students more effectively? Where can I go to find out more?	Keep running list of knowledgeable teachers, survey parents for special expertise, know your local librarians, use the Internet.	
Knowledge of Technology	How can I incorporate computers, calculators, and other technology into my classroom?	Take a computer class, use technological tools in your home life; think of ways to apply that same technology in the classroom.	

Afternoon Matters

On the brim of a straw hat
pond, boys fish barefoot
Mothers sew nearby
the tablecloth picnic half done
Large bees work mauve clover

Soft air, not quite a wind
prods paper boats, pulls
at corn silk hair
The water stirs, and
my guarded heart

A yellow dog jumps for a Frisbee
Children dressed in red, white
and blue watch a mallard duck
make an airplane landing

On this emerald afternoon
on the right hand of reason
it all matters

—Kathleen Gumm

4

The Soul of a Teacher

Never doubt that a small group of thoughtful, committed individuals can change the world. Indeed, it is the only thing that ever has.
—Margaret Mead

What is a soul? Is it some part of ourselves that lives on after our earthly body is gone? Is it a spiritlike quality that sets humans apart from all other creatures? Or perhaps it is life itself, the breath that makes us connected to each other and every other living thing? Many philosophers and great thinkers have attempted to define the "soul" through words and in the end we all take home our own special understanding of exactly what constitutes a soul.

I won't pretend I somehow have a special insight that finally defines the term. My idea of soul is that it is about living by our values and valuing what is uniquely us. It is appreciating what is unique and wonderful about the world. It is about wonder, awe, appreciation, and even to some degree, gratitude. Living for your soul means keeping what you hold dear in your day-to-day actions. Thomas Moore (1992) says, "Many of us spend time and energy trying to be something that we are not. But this is a move against soul, because individuality rises out of the soul as water rises out of the depths of the earth. We are who we are because of the special mix that makes up our soul" (121).

In this chapter I use the concept of the "soul of a teacher" to define the part of our teaching that comes from deep within each of us. It is the part of our teaching that gives us purpose, and it is the beliefs and core values surrounding what we do as teachers. It is, in a sense, the spirit that we bring to the classroom. The chapter is about aiming for some deeper parts of ourselves, parts that are so important and so profound that often we choose to overlook them. It is as if we erect a barricade to keep them from being vulnerable. But in so doing, sometimes we get so far from the core of who we are and what we believe that we actually begin to undermine that which is so crucial to our humanity. I ask you to dig deep, to climb over the protected façade, and ask yourself just a few big questions.

The Role of Values in Teaching

Values are inherent in teaching. There are universal core values and personal principles. The values that fall into the category of universal include such things as integrity, loyalty, courage, and caring. The personal values are those that you hold dear, those by which you live your life as well as by which you live as a teacher. You might believe, for example, that a teacher must bring joy to the classroom. These principles and beliefs live within us whether we choose to pay attention or not. They are essential ingredients in our humanity and are most often noticed when we listen to our conscience. They ultimately affect the way we do things and certainly the way we feel about the things we do.

Examine and express your core beliefs. Unexamined core values can show up when least expected and cause conflict as we go about our daily work. Examining

Part 1: Know Yourself

core values helps us to align the way we teach with our belief systems and to keep our priorities straight as we are confronted by choices. If you know what you believe and why, you will be much less likely to subjugate your belief to less important priorities.

> **What you want for yourself must be congruent with your values.**

It is fun to examine our interests, drives, and knowledge as we have done in the previous chapters, but it is equally important that we keep our values in perspective. I do not believe individuals can lead full, satisfying lives if they negate their conscience and values. What you value must be at the foundation of how you proceed in life. Let's say what you want is to be a great teacher, to win awards, be noticed, have your students excel beyond all expectations. But what you value at your deepest core is a true and whole love of learning.

What you want for yourself must be congruent with your values. Sometimes in our effort to be the best according to others' definition of what that is, we run over our own students' love of learning. No matter how many test scores we might raise or contests we might win, we are left feeling empty because our own values are not driving how we teach.

How many of us know teachers who take pride in the fact that their students are ahead of others in the text or scoring higher than those in other classes? Nevertheless, such teachers seem only temporarily sustained by these small successes and spend time complaining about their lot as a teacher and their students. What actually brought that teacher to teaching? Most probably it was something quite different than racing through materials or charting test scores. Most likely it was a love of people or of subject matter. Perhaps it was a deep belief in the process of learning or the importance of education or a deep love of children. But in the day-to-day process of teaching, other concerns can press in and squeeze out what first led the teacher to teach. Teachers feel pressured to perform in alliance with external priorities. Our values get buried under the business of education. And once those values don't make up the core of how a teacher operates, all the high test scores and quick curriculum coverage will mean nothing at the end of a school year. A teacher will feel empty and wonder why.

How can you get in touch with your deepest values? What questions can you ask that will lead you to know what controls your idea of leading a good life? Begin at the end of your career. The following exercise will help your imagination.

▶ *Exercise 1:*
Retirement Party

Take a few deep breaths, close your eyes and imagine you have a wonderful vantage point at the end of your career. Some students have organized a special event to thank you for your teaching services. At the celebration, people from all aspects of your career stand up at a podium to personally thank you, their teacher, colleague, or employee. They have all come together to recognize the special role you played in the school, in the classroom, in their lives. None of the comments are platitudes or generalizations; they are all very specific comments about you and the impact you have had. Some people share anecdotes, others outline the characteristics for which you are most renowned. Imagine individuals you know standing up and discussing you. See their faces. Imagine stories they could tell about you. Imagine the stories you want them to tell about you.

This exercise will reveal your deepest values. Our values are not always easy to keep in focus. We are human and get distracted by our wants and needs. But when I do this exercise, it puts things back into perspective quite quickly, and I am suddenly strong enough to make important sacrifices to lead the life I most want to lead.

▶ *Exercise 2:*
Eavesdropping Visualization

In this fantasy you overhear a student discussing you as a teacher with a peer or a parent. It is particularly effective if the student was in your class a few years back and is reflecting on how your teaching was a positive influence. The student is saying all the things you would most want to hear if you came upon such a scene, the kinds of things that would swell your chest with pride. Perhaps you helped the student overcome a difficult learning struggle. Perhaps you taught her discipline and organization skills, or spontaneity and a love for learning. What is she saying about you? Be sure she says at least two things you know to be already true and at least two things you wish to be true, but that you might need to work on. Enjoy the eavesdropping.

Taken together, the two exercises tap into the soul of your values and beliefs as a person and a teacher. They reveal a code of ethics by which you may or may not live, but that you certainly value and by which you wish to live. Of course they mean so much more if you can be confident that your choices and actions reflect your values.

Part 1: Know Yourself

▶ *Exercise 3:*
Living Your Priorities Survey

It is easy to believe one way and act in another way if we don't check our day-to-day choices against our belief systems. Take a few moments to look through the following lists. Record in the first column the rank of each item. The highest ranking (1) means you think this item is one of the few most important things you address as a teacher. The lowest ranking (9) means you think this particular item holds little or no value in teaching others. A middle ranking (5) means the item is something that you probably should address as a teacher, but holds no special value to you personally. The lines with *other* are for you to fill in. Perhaps something you spend time on or value is not covered in my list.

> *I believe the most important things a student gets from school are*
>
> ____ ____ multiple perspectives and points of view
> ____ ____ high self-concept and -esteem
> ____ ____ discipline
> ____ ____ structure
> ____ ____ competence in subject area
> ____ ____ memorization of facts associated with subject area
> ____ ____ practice of skills associated with subject area
> ____ ____ note-taking skills
> ____ ____ a love of the subject area and learning
> ____ ____ grades
> ____ ____ motivation to pursue more knowledge and understanding
> ____ ____ fun while learning
> ____ ____ ability to complete a task
> ____ ____ ability to follow directions
> ____ ____ practice communicating what is learned
> ____ ____ ability to express own ideas and opinions
> ____ ____ ability to work with others
> ____ ____ social skills
> ____ ____ citizenship skills
> ____ ____ individual expression
> ____ ____ organization skills
> ____ ____ other (you fill in) _____
> ____ ____ other (you fill in) _____

I believe the most important school-based learning happens through

____ ____ teacher lecture
____ ____ student's verbal expression of ideas
____ ____ student's written expression of ideas
____ ____ note taking
____ ____ work sheets
____ ____ skill practice
____ ____ memorization drills
____ ____ vocabulary associated with subject
____ ____ computer work
____ ____ study for standardized tests
____ ____ using and applying learning to real situations
____ ____ problem solving
____ ____ imagination and creativity
____ ____ student responsibility and independent study
____ ____ ability to work cooperatively in study groups
____ ____ student-determined and -designed study units
____ ____ teacher-designed study units
____ ____ student projects and performance
____ ____ other (you fill in) _____
____ ____ other (you fill in) _____

I believe the most important things I do as a teacher are

____ ____ support the district and school administration in their priorities
____ ____ assign grades
____ ____ test
____ ____ model skills and learning
____ ____ give feedback to students on their specific learning progress
____ ____ report to parents and students on overall progress
____ ____ teach (lecture, visuals, etc.) a lesson
____ ____ gives students practice in a portion of a lesson
____ ____ assign homework
____ ____ motivate my students
____ ____ help my students appreciate the relevance of what they are learning
____ ____ complete the textbook within the school calendar
____ ____ prepare students for standardized tests
____ ____ have fun with my students
____ ____ listen to my students
____ ____ other (you fill in) _____
____ ____ other (you fill in) _____

Part 1: Know Yourself

Cover the first column of numbers with a piece of paper. In the second column, note the number of times in the last teaching week you addressed that particular issue or skill. Recall specific instances when you focused on each. If you cannot recall specifics, it may be because you do not address that issue regularly. If you were able to think of more than five or six occasions, then you are probably oriented to addressing that particular issue. If you could not name more than one, then you are probably not oriented to addressing that issue.

Now look at both columns. Note any items you marked as a 5 to 9 (medium to low priority) but could remember addressing more than six times. Note any items you marked as 1 to 3 (very high priority) but could remember addressing no more than one time in the last week. The idea of this survey is to check whether your teaching is aligned with your priorities. When you find discrepancies between what you actually pursue in your classroom and what you believe you should pursue, it is time to reorganize how you spend your time.

▶ *Exercise 4:*
Paradigms to Build or Challenge

Paradigms are beliefs or preconditioned ways of looking at something. Knowing your preconceived ideas about school, students, and learning is important. If you have paradigms that undermine your success as a teacher, then you need to challenge them and re-create your thinking.

One common teaching paradigm is left over from the days when adults believed "children should be seen and not heard." My sister loves to tell the story about the poster displayed high above the main office desk that said, "If you are talking, you are not learning." My sister and I have giggled over this poster. We are both talker-thinkers. We hash through our thoughts and learn as we converse, sometimes not even listening to each other. I had a student once who could not learn unless she was talking! Jocelyn was a very bright child who happened to think out loud. She would propose problems and then propose solutions. She would work through the logic of each of her ideas until she arrived at a conclusion or solution. It annoyed other students who could not think when she was thinking so loudly, but most certainly that school poster did not apply to Jocelyn! It was important for me to recognize Jocelyn's style of learning and to find appropriate ways for her to continue learning without disturbing other students. But if I stayed with the paradigm communicated in that school poster, no doubt Jocelyn would have failed miserably as my student. I value helping a student to learn and succeed much more than I value a silent classroom.

Do you believe, really believe, all students can learn? Did you know the brain cannot help but learn? Perhaps certain brains simply choose not to buy what we teachers are selling. If you change your paradigm from "some students cannot learn" to "all students are constantly learning," then your job as teacher changes drastically. Can you see that? If some students simply cannot learn, then you are just baby-sitting them and teaching the rest. If all students are constantly learning, then suddenly you might have to work harder to get into their heads and find out what so captivates them there that they cannot focus on what you offer.

> *I value helping a student to learn and succeed much more than I value a silent classroom.*

How about this paradigm: "If I do not help all of my students to learn, then I have failed." How many teachers feel this at the deepest level? We know we are feeling it because at the end of the school year we can remember only the one student we could not reach. It was Mother Teresa who said, "If you can't feed a hundred people, then feed just one." While I advocate never giving up on a student, I also advocate remembering and enjoying those that you do reach. The more time and energy you spend focusing on your success as a teacher, the more positive energy you will have to devote to the more difficult cases for you to crack. Teaching can be a real burnout profession if you seldom pay attention to the rewards.

Perhaps you have a few paradigms that get in the way of your teaching. How about, "It is best to teach in the same way others teach"; "Learning is boring, hard work"; "Learning only happens step-by-step." What other paradigms can you think of? Think of the beliefs that you notice sticking in your soul; list some of them. Then in your journal or your support group, explore how it is limiting or enhancing your teaching. In what ways does the paradigm impede your effectiveness? In what ways does it enhance it? Is it damaging or helpful overall? In what ways can you change it, if necessary, to a more helpful and enlightening paradigm?

▶ *Exercise 5:*
Your Special Gift or Purpose

As I have said, every teacher is different just as every student is different. What makes us special as teachers is individual to each teacher. As you have moved through the first chapters of this book, I hope you have come to see some of the qualities that make you unique and special as a teacher. I encourage you to value and express your unique qualities.

You are not like any other teacher. Can you explain why not? It may be easiest to begin by explaining what you are not. If you can put into words everything you aren't, then explaining what you are becomes easier. Try this exercise with some friends or a support group. Finish sentences such as the following:

- I am not a teacher who
- I am not likely to do this in the classroom
- I will never believe this about students

From that exercise you can build statements about who you are. Put them into words or pictures so that you have something concrete to hold onto.

Can you identify the one main thing, the overriding unique purpose that you bring to teaching and the classroom? It is important to give it a name. To label it allows you to easily recall and protect it. If you allow your unique purpose to go unexpressed it is likely to get washed away in the tide of teacher expectations that surround you. Express it.

Ways to Support and Protect Your Values

So, you work hard at getting in touch with your deepest beliefs and values about school and learning and students, what do you do with this knowledge? You protect it. As I said in the beginning of the chapter, "What you value must be at the foundation of how you proceed in life."

> *Find ways for your students to develop and express opinions, every week, every day.*

Step 1: To keep your values and beliefs safe, know what they are. I hope this chapter has helped you get closer to your core beliefs.

Step 2: Visit your beliefs and values regularly. Visit your beliefs by keeping them somewhere accessible. Make it a regular practice to review what you believe. In the Teacher Manifesto exercise, I encourage you to create a creed that gives you a method for touching base with your core values regularly. Develop a creed to help you hold your beliefs in special esteem.

Step 3: Live your values and beliefs every day to keep them strong. Practice what you preach, as they say. If you realize that you seldom address or encourage something you esteem, such as student opinion and thought, work on it. Begin to find ways for your students to develop and express opinions, every week, every day, if possible.

Step 4: Never undermine what you believe. If you value all students and believe they all can learn, don't stand numb allowing other teachers to tell you about students who can't learn. Interrupt, or leave, or find a diplomatic way of letting the teacher know the talk is not helpful. If you believe parents are important to the educational process, don't discourage parent visits to the classroom or talk negatively about parents with other teachers. These seemingly small digressions will slowly eat away at your principles. You don't need to become a preacher for your values, but do not subjugate them in the name of peace. You are capable of being a quiet leader and causing great change to occur.

Hiatus

*For lack of a bank
or bend in the road
some island of blue on white sand*

*A room of pale green
wide windows, a desk
overlooking a thousand words*

*painted in seashell
water and breeze
daring the currents, the shore*

*braving blank pages
and this wide open sea
to find the artist in me.*

—Kathleen Gumm

Part 2

Develop a Plan

5

A Teaching Ideal

A "scientifically" brought-up child would be a pitiable monster. A "scientific" friendship would be as cold as a chess problem. "Scientific" teaching, even of scientific subjects, will be inadequate as long as both teachers and pupils are human beings. Teaching is not like inducing a chemical reaction: it is much more like painting a picture or making a piece of music . . . You must throw your heart into it, you must realize that it cannot all be done by formulas, or you will spoil your work, and your pupils, and yourself.

—Gilbert Highet in *The Art of Teaching*

We, as teachers, are advised often what makes a great teacher. We are advised from studies being done on teaching. We are advised by parents and other teachers. Even our own students tell us who teaches well. Sometimes we are lucky enough that they point at us. Great feeling.

Everyone has an opinion about great or good and especially about bad teaching. Perhaps because we have all attended school, we all have opinions about what we experienced there, in those long hallways and desk-filled rooms. Some of us experienced enthusiastic, supercharged teachers. Others experienced intense, serious, book-driven learning. Some have experienced both. All of us have developed ideas about what worked and what didn't. Or, at the very least, all of us know what we liked and didn't like.

This book is about self-directed improvement, and essential to your drive and motivation is your personal concept of great teaching. This chapter is about clarifying your vision of what makes a teacher great. The activities involve searching through your own perceptions as well as the perceptions of others.

▶ Exercise 1:
Brainstorm Qualities That Make a Great Teacher

This exercise helps participants identify some of the universal principles inherent in quality teaching. You can do this exercise on your own, but it is so much more fun and useful if you involve a group of people. They don't need to be teachers; they just must have attended school. Ask your group the following questions: When were times that you really felt you were learning, understanding, or achieving in the classroom? What was your teacher doing or not doing that led to this success? What was the environment like? (How did it look? Sound? Feel?) What did other students think of this environment and this teacher? Talk freely about your varied experiences for a few minutes.

Now, together or alone, list qualities of a great teacher. Keep listing for more than ten minutes, even if you hit a slump and have no more ideas. Remember one of the amazing things about brainstorming is that the more specific information begins to flow right after that slump. Often people start with "A good teacher is thoughtful, knowledgeable, enthusiastic, wise, patient" until they run out of platitudes and hit the slump. Then they begin digging for the nuts and bolts: A good teacher is extremely organized, eccentric, tells a good joke, sets the room up so students participate, surrounds students with stimulating things and ideas, demands students work above their present level, treats students as special human beings with terrific learning qualities, loves the job, handles crisis as if born in a war zone, forces students to think and work, is structured so students know what comes next, has twenty-three different ways of presenting the same information.

Part 2: Develop a Plan

Understand that most members of your group will never have actually known one teacher with all of the qualities you list. The qualities will be a compilation of the many different teachers you have known or experienced. In addition, sometimes the qualities will appear to completely contradict one another. "You always know what comes next" vs. "You never know what comes next." "Makes the room quiet and comfortable so you love to be there and you can concentrate" vs. "Makes the room actually explode with stimulating ideas and objects." Certain qualities seem universally to represent good teaching: enthusiasm for the subject matter, challenging students to think, asking good probing questions, fairness. Many other qualities are quite arguable either way.

> **Certain qualities seem universally to represent good teaching.**

One teacher at a school where I taught enrichment was quite unusual. "Miss Marple" was set in her ways and opinionated, and she hated to work with other teachers or even within the system. When a standardized curriculum was set up she inevitably strayed from the plans. The other teachers and staff found her frustrating and irresponsible.

Miss Marple's students thought she was marvelous. They understood she wasn't the standard fare, but they loved her eccentricities. Miss Marple always surrounded her students with fascinating subject matter and had weird objects dangled throughout her classroom. Lessons mostly strayed off track and students would end up discussing subjects that seemed unrelated. Everything was a new adventure.

And her students were productive. They produced wonderful writing ideas and artwork. They loved mathematical puzzles and games. I found them eager to attempt new and even difficult subject matter. Many students in that class were highly accomplished at divergent thinking.

Should all teachers begin making their classrooms look like the attics of museums and galleries, as Miss Marple did? Should they subvert the standard learning fare and create an environment of earthy strangeness that focuses on writing and artwork? I have to say Miss Marple's abilities could not be completely discounted. Those students who were lucky enough to have her for one year walked away with some very special learning gifts indeed.

But I don't advocate trashing the curriculum just to produce excellent teachers. I support a more balanced approach to instruction. I tell about this teacher because I want to point out that good teaching qualities vary with the teaching style of individual teachers. When you have completed a list of teaching qualities, the contradictory qualities generally reflect teaching styles.

A Teaching Ideal

Examine the list of teaching qualities that you (and friends) created:

1. ✔ Put check marks next to all of the qualities you exhibit as a teacher.

2. ★ Put stars next to three to five qualities you would identify as your strengths.

3. ○ Circle two to three qualities you most wish to develop.

▶ *Exercise 2:*
Thank You, Thank You!

A few summers ago I had the privilege of touring the Salk Institute in San Diego with a group of teachers and administrators. The Salk Institute is an inspirational structure, perched on the edge of a hilltop and inclined toward the sky. Every detail of the institute's architecture suggests looking toward the future. The long courtyard leads to higher and higher vistas with the final view extending out to the Pacific Ocean. Clean lines, rippling water, contemplative vistas are all integrated into the design of the building. It is a commanding structure.

Through the institute pass some of the finest scientific minds of our time. People selected to work there are leading scientists and thinkers. The institute is a tribute to scientific research and has supported many Nobel Laureates in their quest for knowledge.

During our tour one teacher commented on how fabulous it would feel to work at the institute. A second teacher paused thoughtfully. "I wouldn't want to work here myself. But I would give anything to know one of my students made it here!" One synchronized hum of approval from the entire group made me realize the true rewards of teaching. We all wanted to be the teacher who launches a student into Salk Institute.

So often our students do reach great heights. How often do they acknowledge the teachers who helped them on their path? What greater gift can a teacher receive than acknowledgment from a student who has succeeded and believed the teacher played some role in that success? Perhaps we should hold a teacher protest with signs and placards that demand acknowledgment. Then again . . . how many teachers have you thanked?

Write a thank-you note to a past teacher. Look back on your school experiences. Can you remember one teacher who influenced and helped you? It does not matter if you are unable to reach that teacher. Write the note as if you have been handed an opportunity to reach out and thank this person. Be very specific in the note. Tell the teacher exactly what he or she did to help you learn and why it was effective for you.

Part 2: Develop a Plan

> **Teachers ... who made a difference in your learning ... are mentors for your future teaching.**

My sister took this advice and wrote a thank-you note to a teacher she had had twenty years before. She managed to come up with an address and mail the note. Sadly, he had passed away just one month before, but his widow was so grateful to hear such wonderful stories and thoughts about her spouse from one of his early students! She immediately called my sister to thank her for the special gift.

This assignment is very cathartic. If I were giving you grades, you would get an "A" if you locate the teacher and send the note! Wouldn't it be wonderful if all ex-students did this exercise? I wish you all good karma back from every thank-you note you send.

Now, as nice as it is to imagine teachers everywhere contacting their mentors from the past, I hope you also gain insight from this exercise. I hope sending a thank-you helps you identify specific teaching qualities, attitudes, and practices that mattered most to you as a student. Those teachers from your past who made a difference in your learning, no matter how small, are mentors for your future teaching. Remember them. Thank them. Emulate them.

▶ *Exercise 3:*
Emulate the Masters

If I sent you into the staff lounge and told you, "For each teacher in this room you must think of at least one outstanding teacher quality, behavior, or habit," you might smile or grimace, depending on your campus. Some faculties are filled with interesting, exciting, talented teachers who offer you a multitude of identifiable strengths. Some faculties are made up of many burnt-out teachers who survive day to day.

Nonetheless, I encourage you to look carefully whatever your circumstances. That burnt-out teacher who has a different philosophy from yours may well have some hidden talent you never stopped to consider. Being burnt out is often a sign of caring immensely about a job at some point and not receiving the support needed to keep enthusiasm. Many teachers on your faculty may have hidden special talents that your personal interest can reignite.

Truth is, most teachers have some quality worth emulating. It might be as small as the way they trim their bulletin boards or as large as the ability to motivate huge groups of students, but it is a quality. Rest assured, I am not asking you to go around copying every other teacher. I just think it is well worth your while to take a look. You will realize the many elements you value in teaching and you will realize there is a wealth of information sitting in your staff lounge. When you get to the chapter on finding resources to reach your goals, you will start at your school with teachers you identify in this exercise.

Make a chart with the headings "Teacher," "Phone Number," "Talent/Strength/Skill." Fill in at least five names of teachers accessible to you. The more teachers you list the more resources at your fingertips.

▶ *Exercise 4:*
In a Perfect World

In schools, teachers often spend time complaining and worrying about many things. They complain about classroom size and the number of students they are expected to teach. They worry about home environments and the problems students bring to school. They complain about administration's over-control or lack of direction. Teachers fret over materials, supplies, and the school environment. They worry that they don't know enough or have too little experience, or that they are burnt out and out of touch.

Some or all of these things might bother you. Or perhaps you have a different set of struggles and limitations. In this exercise I want you to imagine what teaching would be like if all of your teaching fears had been addressed. Everything that bothers you is eradicated and all your needs are met in your perfect teaching world. What is your teaching world like? What does it look like? Sound like? Feel like? How are you teaching? Do you move about the room or stay in one place? In what activities are you involved? What do you no longer need to do? What are you doing well? How do you feel? Really let reality go!

When you are finished with this fantasy, ponder your list. Did your subconscious mind surprise you with ideas you had not considered? Were there any details that you could create without much effort, training, or materials? Were there details that seemed obtainable even though they might require more of your time or effort? Which details seemed beyond realistic expectations?

Now ponder the bigger picture. What three things in this perfect teaching world would *most greatly and positively influence your present teaching life?* They are your priorities. As you move into planning and goal setting, keep these priorities in mind. If some are wonderful fantasies that you do not believe you can ever obtain, share them with your support group or some creative friends. Ask them to help you solve the impossible. Hold a short brainstorm session aimed at finding a way to make all your teaching dreams come true. You might be surprised at the multitude of elements that you can actually make happen if you think creatively and open your mind to the possibilities. The possible takes a little time to accomplish. The impossible simply takes a little longer.

Part 2: Develop a Plan

▶ *Exercise 5:*
The Framework for Teaching

Charlotte Danielson's (1996) *Enhancing Professional Practice* is a wonderful resource for teachers on a professional growth journey. Danielson lists teacher skills and attributes identified in *The Framework for Teaching,* a teacher training framework designed by the Educational Testing Service. For more detailed and sequential use of the Praxis III model I recommend using Danielson's book or attending a workshop. Whether you use the entire framework or not, it is useful to keep in mind the four domains of professional responsibility highlighted by *The Framework for Teaching*. The chart on page 57 has a square for each domain. Use the chart to identify one goal in each domain.

Conclusion: The Beauty of Never Getting There

I name this chapter "A Teaching Ideal" rather than "The Perfect Teacher" for a reason. Perfection is not ideal. Perfection means you have reached the end of the path; there is no place to go except down. Who needs that kind of pressure? It is so much more conducive to a learning environment to be a learning person, someone who always has room to grow and an upward direction to seek. I wish for you and me and all teachers that we are never "perfect" and always progressing toward our ideal!

The Framework for Teaching Domain Goals

Domain 1: Planning and Preparation This domain covers a teacher's preparation, including knowledge of students, resources and subject matter, and design of instruction and assessment.	**Domain 2: The Classroom Environment** This domain covers the teacher's classroom management, classroom arrangement, and the social cultural climate.
Domain 3: Instruction This domain covers the teacher's instruction of students including clarity, questioning, feedback, and regrouping ability.	**Domain 4: Professional Responsibilities** This domain is about the teacher's ability to grow and develop, to show leadership, to communicate with families, and to keep good records.

Perfectionist

When the moon swallows
the sun leaving long ticking
hours where sleep does not come
Every ribbon of me wanting to think
myself a champion

and to still this voice so far away
come when I was long-legged young
to the pockets of night

where I lie and make long lists; all the things
I didn't do that day, and the things I did
and should have done—better

When I rise with the sun
at tall windows overlooking dawns
familiar sights, the air smelling of cool
and want; of the weather in my face

I no longer wonder
why I'm black and blue.

Hey! I'm good at this

—Kathleen Gumm

6

A Teacher Manifesto

I TEACH THEREFORE I AM

There is a story in which a teacher fills a bucket with rocks and then asks his students if it is full. They all nod yes in unison. Then he brings up a bag of gravel and fills the bucket more. Again he asks, "Is it full?" The students grin, because they begin to understand the contradiction and one or two answer, "No, not yet." Then he brings up a bag of sand and fills the bucket even more. "Now is it full?" he asks. The students hesitate, then scream, "No!" in unison. The teacher then pulls out a container of water and begins to fill the bucket even more.

"What does this illustrate about time?" the teacher asks. One student eagerly responds, "You can always find more space and time." The teacher suggests a different perspective, "It also shows us that if we don't put in the big things first, we won't be able to fit them in later."

Part 2: Develop a Plan

When you plan for professional development you are likely to become caught up in all the details and specifics. Doesn't that make it impossible to keep you focused on the big picture, the things you value most? Stephen Covey (1989) recommends developing a purposeful mission statement and living by it. It gives you a solid foundation for choosing what is most important and putting it first. As he says, you need "a clear sense of direction and value, a burning 'yes!' inside that makes it possible to say 'no' to other things" (149).

When I first taught full time in an elementary classroom my district was in the middle of a huge budget crunch. The pressure was mounting throughout the district. During staff meetings, a huge emphasis was placed on getting absentee notes from our parents. Unless students had a note from home, the state would not pay for students who had been absent. Because many of my parents did not speak English, I had to stress the importance of the attendance notes with my students, hoping they would carry the messages home. Every day I would sequester the students who had been absent and ask them for the notes from their parents. I would discuss the importance of bringing the notes and stress that I might have to take away privileges if they did not bring in their notes.

> *The student ranks higher than any district paperwork pressures.*

My frustration was building with one particular student. Aaron was regularly absent and often returned to school without notes. It was like pulling teeth to get him to remember. One particularly harried day, Aaron came in late and without a note for his previous absence. I scolded him and took away his recess. In the chaos of getting the day started and dealing with the various paperwork and testing pressures of the day, I failed to notice the frozen look on his face. Later in the morning, at a quiet moment, another student pulled me to the side to inform me that the police had come to Aaron's home the previous night to take his father away. Aaron's mother had left, too, and not yet returned. The fact that he had shown up for school at all was a bit of a miracle! Needless to say, I felt racked with guilt over my response, given the drama of Aaron's predicament. He had come to school despite all of this!

I immediately realized how the stress and grind of day-to-day teaching and pressure from outside sources can have a negative impact on my true core values as a teacher. I vowed to work harder at keeping the most important things uppermost in my mind. For me, the student ranks higher than any district paperwork pressures. I don't advocate casting aside the paperwork. Paperwork is part of teacher work. I strive only to keep the paperwork in its proper pecking order. Our motivations as teachers, our belief systems about learning, our desire to make a difference in the lives of others should not be held hostage to the other more mundane aspects of the job of teaching.

▶ *Exercise 1:*
Creating a Clear Vision

If you can see it in your imagination, then you can make it happen. If you cannot visualize a result, then you may struggle to get there. Some inventors fully create imaginary machinery, then test it in their minds to see if it works before ever building a model! Can you do this for your classroom?

Create a vision for the end of your school year. It has been an ideal school year and today is the last day. Students are packing up to leave your classroom. With what are they leaving? What did they gain from being in your company for a year? As you look around the room, what do you see in each student's eyes and heart? Is what you see and feel all related to the curriculum, or is there something more? How does it feel to see them so successful and ready to move on?

Make this vision as clear and concise as you can. The more exact you can be, the better your chances of achieving that ideal at the end of the year. Hold onto this picture in your mind. Bring it back up from time to time. It is your visual mantra.

▶ *Exercise 2:*
Creating a Teacher Manifesto

Design a statement of belief about teaching. You can call it a pledge or a creed. Or you can call it your personal teaching promise. Whatever you call it, the purpose of this statement is to inspire you to keep uppermost in your mind your reasons for teaching. If you look at or listen to this manifesto, it should give you a sense of importance about what you strive to do as a teacher. It should bring to mind your vision of your students at the end of the year. It should make you feel strong and special inside. It should give you almost that same patriotic burst of pride that often comes with the first refrain of our national anthem.

Look over the journal, notes, and pictures that you have been keeping since chapter 1. Talk over your priorities and beliefs with your support group. Think about your realizations from the exercises. Look for three things: emotional twinges, idea patterns, and personal "ahas," and list them in a chart or other format so you can study them when you are through.

Part 2: Develop a Plan

Emotional twinges might have occurred when you imagined your retirement party or when you imagined a student talking about you. The pang you may have felt comes from deep within. It is your subconscious quest for recognition reaching out to your conscious self, asking you to take note of the things that are most important to you. You may have felt sadness for things you have ignored. You may have felt pride in the things you already live by. The emotional connection is an important ingredient in any attempt to grow and change. Keep track of the ideas in which you feel emotionally invested.

> **You need to dream big; big dreams are what make our blood flow.**

Idea patterns are concepts, qualities, and thoughts that repeated themselves more than once. Perhaps in your teacher brainstorm list, in your thank-you note, and in your ideal day, you notice a particular teaching quality. Ideas that came up in more than one exercise are patterns of thought. Take note because these may be areas you wish to keep on the forefront of your mind.

Finally, "ahas" are those self-realization kicks in the head that occur when we answer a question and suddenly reveal something that was not clear before. Did you, as you were discussing the color of your teaching or as you described your perfect teaching day, suddenly feel that leap of understanding? An aha comes at the peak of any struggle with understanding. When the light suddenly shines where it was dark we have experienced an aha. If you had some revelations during the previous chapters, welcome to the club. Most teachers find the activities open their minds to something they had not considered before.

Manifestos are very personalized. You will put together and select the style, arrangement, words, and pictures. Some folks prefer an outline format with key points made and details under each key point. Some prefer a musical rendition of inspirational compositions. Others like a short, to-the-point paragraph. Still others might choose poetry, a collage, or perhaps a video presentation. What is most important is that it is comfortable and sincere, and that you own it. It does not need to be your pictures, music, or words. It may be that you collect quotations, pictures, or songs that hold personal meaning.

One other important aspect of the creed is that it is "lofty." Human beings are not moved to accomplish minimal goals, which explains why the dust on top of the overhead fan does not attract your attention when housecleaning. You need to dream big; big dreams are what make our blood flow. Without the bigger ideas we wander aimlessly in small seas rather than striving. So don't write a manifesto filled with small ideas. Focus on the lofty thoughts that make your heart jump.

Some concepts you may want to communicate in your teacher creed are listed below. Include what you want to keep on the forefront of your mind and heart. Remember less is often better than more. Keep it simple.

Your vision of your students at the end of the year

Your emotional twinges, your patterns, and your ahas

Your beliefs about learning and about students

Your most important overriding goals as a teacher

The strengths you bring to the classroom

Your thoughts and attitudes about the subject matter that you teach

Your personal teaching style

A statement about teaching or students that might inspire or motivate you to do your best

Any promises you wish to make to yourself and your students

However you choose to present your creed, the most important thing is that you make it personal, inspirational, and honest. Do not put down promises or ideas that you do not believe in.

Many teachers will use inspirations from posters they already have hanging in their classrooms to begin. Those posters are very like what I am advocating here, except often we hang those posters for our students and then forget they are there. Or we look at them and enjoy them, but neglect to give special attention to their meaning on a regular basis. The difference between inspirational posters and a teacher creed lies in the attention we devote to the meaning behind the words.

Example Manifestos

1. **A Photograph Collage:** Imagine many photos of students engaged in hands-on activities with expressions of interest and excitement on their faces. Words cut from magazines and advertisements adorn the collage with ideas like "Fun and exciting!" "Discover your world!" and "Together we learn." Surrounding that visual theme are photographs of adults engaged in exciting careers: astronauts, musicians, scientists, and architects.
2. **A Photograph or Video Collage:** People are talking about the difference school has made in their lives, about the importance of teachers. Each photograph tells a different story about what a student gained from a year in your classroom. These could be mythological people, inventions from your vision of the end of the year.

Part 2: Develop a Plan

3. **A Written Statement:** Imagine a large poster board with the words, "I am a teacher who strives to reach every student. I believe every student has a special outlook, learning style, and gift to bring to the classroom. It is my job to help them discover their unique potential. Their struggles are my struggles and I have not succeeded until my students have felt a measure of success. I demonstrate this attitude in the way that I plan my lessons and carry out my instruction. I am flexible when my students need flexibility. I am open to trying new ways to teach. I am constantly striving to better understand and work with each and every student. I believe in them." Or the words, "I am not your mother or father. I am your teacher. I am here to challenge you to learn and to reach. It is most important to me that you reach for your highest potential. Sometimes, that means we will experience frustration and confusion. I understand those emotions. I will not accept giving up. Stick to the job and I will stick with you."

   > *I will not accept giving up.*

4. **A Short Statement of Belief:** Learning is fun! Learning is hard work and fun! Learning means listening and talking, looking and touching, feeling and showing. Teaching means helping others discover the fun of learning.

5. **A Musical Creed:** Create a tape filled with songs that hold special meaning to you as a teacher and that are musically appealing. Some of the lyrics may be about heroic role models ("Wind beneath My Wings," "I Believe I Can Fly"). Other pieces may be instrumental but evoke the feelings and beliefs you hold dear or that make you feel effective and powerful as a teacher (perhaps the theme from *Rocky* or a classical piece of music).

6. **A Video Clip:** Combine famous teaching moments from inspirational movies with your own classroom moments that you have been lucky enough to capture on tape. Add clips of a few of your past students who were willing to make statements about the difference you made in their lives.

7. **Selection of Statements:** Create five positive affirmations about the importance of being a teacher and place them in strategic locations throughout your home and classroom. Change the locations, format, and coloring of the statements regularly so that they do not blend in with the surroundings and become forgotten. Separating your manifesto into parts helps individual parts remain important and foremost in your consciousness.

8. **Letters and Praise:** Post letters from students or parents of your students. The letters should express the role you have played in their lives and remind you why you teach. Reread them regularly and feel proud of what you have accomplished.
9. **Student Made:** Believe in the importance of student choice and decision making in learning. Ask students to brainstorm five main things about teaching that you should keep first in your mind. Then display those five points where you and your students see them every day.

▶ *Exercise 3:*
Using Your Creed

Make it a practice to give your creed uninterrupted attention every day. Look at it, listen to it, or read it aloud to yourself and believe in it. Think of it as a personal reminder about what you strive for. It is a way to keep conscious of your teaching principles. As you begin to work on individual goals, keep one eye on the bigger picture, the things you most value about your work as a teacher. The creed is your source for that reminder.

> *Give your creed uninterrupted attention every day.*

Affirmations are a catalyst for growth and change. Positive personal statements read or said aloud have been shown to affect the internal messages the reader gives herself. Most of us have a huge selection of critical or negative affirmations that we use consciously or unconsciously to undermine our confidence or confirm our lack of confidence. We say things to ourselves like, "You idiot, I can't believe you did that" or "What is the matter with you?" Often these negative personal statements are left over from childhood. When we counteract negative statements by using self-affirmations, we counteract the damage negative statements do to our self-esteem and confidence.

Think of your teacher manifesto as a positive self-affirmation. Use it as a foundation. Create it as an image in your mind. If you imagine your manifesto in action, you can make it happen. Let it influence your subconscious and your conscious so that you are consistently striving to be the teacher you can admire and respect. Make it balance out and finally negate the less-than-stellar comments of your inner critic.

Once you feel confident and comfortable with your creed, make it public. Display it, play it, or read it to your class. Let your students and other teachers know what it is you aim to achieve. They will support you in your quest for success.

Exercise 4:
Revising Your Manifesto

Define and use your creed (privately or otherwise) for a short period (one month or two) before making any revisions. Read it, experience it, and imagine it every day. You will sense after a short trial period which parts work for you and which are inadequate. It is very typical that revisions will be needed because as you work with your creed and on your professional growth plan, you will hone the ideas that best fit you.

There is no rule of thumb for revisions. You are on a path of professional growth and your creed will probably change as you change. You might start a poster or collage, then add more as you hone your vision. Certain fundamental principles about your teaching and learning beliefs will remain a part of your creed throughout every revision. Once your creed feels solid, review and revise it once each year as an exercise in self-awareness.

Questions to ask when you are revising your creed:

1. When I read, hear, or look at my creed, am I inspired to do my best as a teacher? Sometimes your creed will be essentially fine, but if you have used it for a long time it may feel worn. Create fresh words or a fresh direction that will reinstill the emotional connection you have with the creed, or reproduce your creed in a new format (pictures or music, posters, or a poem).

2. Can I imagine it? Is my mind's-eye view of what I most want to happen in my classroom clear and purposeful? If you can imagine it you will be able to communicate what it is you hope to achieve to yourself and your students. Many successful people will tell you they visualize their success before attaining it. They know exactly what the end is going to look like because they have imagined it in their heads a million times.

3. Are my goals, beliefs and priorities the same as when I wrote the creed? Perhaps over the last year you have found a different goal or ideal that you need to express in your creed.

4. Do I still feel connected to my inner resources and strengths, and to my style as a teacher? Go back through some of the self-awareness exercises in earlier chapters to reconnect to some of the ideas they produced if you are now feeling remote from your original aspirations.

5. Do I review my creed often or is the format too inconvenient or too long for regular perusal? Perhaps you need to make it more accessible so that you use it regularly. It is not useful if you do not actually review it. Better to produce something short that you truly use, than a long complex oath that you never look at.

Behind the Camera

We've collected all the children
for a group picture
They face the camera
brown twisted and limb scratched
like young trees in the wood
eager to be moving with breeze

We see ourselves

See it in the shape of a nose
See it in the color of an eye
The length of a leg

And we remember when we were young
Cousins and brothers and sisters
side by side

When we possessed the smell of lake
the scent of pine
Long bracelets of summer
when we were golden linked.

The picture taken, the children flee
to grow up
into you
to grow up
into me.

—Kathleen Gumm

7

Self-Observation

All my life, I always wanted to be somebody. Now I see that I should have been more specific.

—Jane Wagner

Self-Observation

One key to changing anything successfully is to first understand clearly and absolutely that which you intend to change. There is a story about a grandfather who was watching his granddaughter repeatedly dig holes in the dirt. Nearby were several jars of plant cuttings that had roots and were ready to be planted. The granddaughter was experiencing some measure of frustration with her work. She would dig a hole, then grunt and grumble, fill it in and dig another hole. Grandfather determined his help was needed and stepped in, as any well-meaning grandfather would. "Here, honey," he said. "What you need to do is dig the hole, then put the root part of the cutting into the hole, then fill around the root cutting with dirt and give it just a little water." He demonstrated carefully the planting of one of the plant clippings. His granddaughter listened, then repeated his actions with the remaining plant clippings. "There," he said to her. "Didn't you do a good job planting those clippings?"

> *One key to changing anything successfully is to first understand clearly and absolutely that which you intend to change.*

"Yes," she answered. "But I still didn't find any worms for fish bait."

Sometimes we are so quick to plow into setting goals and making them work that we neglect taking the time to clearly see and understand our present course of direction. We end up addressing big things when perhaps only little changes are needed.

I am a lazy sugarholic. I seldom get up the energy to go out shopping for something sweet, but if it is available, I eat it. For years I would grumble about my up-and-down weight gain. I would put myself on strange diets, then follow up with huge binges on all the sweets I love. I always kept a back-up supply in the house. It never occurred to me just to limit the number of sweets in my house and skip the crazy diets, until I married my husband. He does not like sweets in the house. We seldom keep "extras" in the house. Occasionally when I am out shopping, I will pick up something sweet to eat, but I am no longer on a binge cycle and I never diet anymore. With less effort, I am a relatively steady size eight.

My approach might not be your diet answer, but it is important that before embarking on any plan of action, we first spend some time observing and understanding the behavior we want to change. Everyone is an individual; there is no one problem–one solution recipe that works for all people. Self-observation devotes time and energy to our individuality. It means looking closely to understand fully our own successes and roadblocks. We may find more direct routes to fixing a problem than we previously imagined.

Part 2: Develop a Plan

What about professional development? It is certainly more varied and complex than changing one of our habits. Nevertheless, I think perhaps the most crucial steps happen before you take any steps toward your goals. The first step, self-reflection, I have covered; it is asking deep questions and getting in touch with what is inside. The next step is self-observation, taking a close look at your teacher actions and behaviors. It is during self-observation that you gain the quality insight about where you need to go and how best to get there. Your display space, journal, and support group can act as vehicles for self-observation and self-reflection. By sitting down daily or weekly to evaluate and discuss what is happening in your life as a teacher, you are automatically encouraging self-observation. This chapter is about enhancing your current self-observation repertoire with four self-observation and evaluation techniques.

> *Self-observation is the measure-twice part of your self-development plan.*

You might be tempted to skip this part and go right on into the action plan. As human beings, we find it difficult not to get straight to the goal setting. Our brains are built for problem solving, not patience and observation. We want to put check marks next to all the things we've completed, not add more things to the list! Nevertheless, I cannot stress to you how helpful this chapter will be to the success of your overall plan. In fact, it is so important I think it should be the first step in meeting the professional development goals you began to set in the self-reflection process.

My father often says, "When you start any building project, measure twice, cut once." Self-observation is the measure-twice part of your self-development plan. Without it you may find yourself needlessly starting over and over on your goals, when perhaps you have aimed your arrows at the least helpful target.

So, how do you get started on self-observation? First and foremost, map out a two-week (or more) section on your calendar. During these two weeks you are not to work on any of the exercises from earlier chapters, nor are you to move on to work on subsequent chapters. You may continue only making daily entries in your journal, meeting daily with your support group, and you may begin work in this chapter. Ideally, all members of your support group will be at the same point, and you all can share and observe regularly during this two-week period.

The point of this observation period is to get the clearest picture possible of where you are now. There is no one "right" place to be. At the end of your self-observation period you may find you have strengths and weaknesses you had not previously recognized.

If you are a perfectionist and highly self-critical, this two-week exercise is going to be difficult. But this exercise is not the time to become defensive or self-depreciating. Your foremost priority is to ignore your critical voice and be an objective observer, which is why the journal and support group will be so helpful. Use them as a source for self-reflection rather than self-beating. This time is for looking openly at your teaching self, examining how you spend your work time, looking closely at the high points and low points of your day, and asking yourself honestly and sincerely, "How am I doing?"

▶ *Exercise 1:*
Observation to Discover

Your first observation assignment is passive. Spend three to seven days with a raised awareness about your behavior. Heighten your awareness by using the following methods:

Journal Writing

For at least three school days write a statement or notes about your actions and feelings at the end of each activity. Write just before the start of class about how you spent your preparatory time. Write during recess or breaks about how you spent your class time prior to the break. At the conclusion of the day, note what you did between the previous break and the end of school. You might cover the actions you took, the feelings you had, and your judgment about how things went. What went well? What frustrated you? Do not spend time thinking of solutions or changes. Focus only on what you are currently doing. This exercise may seem like an abundance of work to add to your schedule, but trust the process and do it. The time is very short, only three days, and it will give you a lifetime's worth of information about your teaching. If you simply cannot bring yourself to write, at the very least, stop and mentally review.

Support Partner or Group

Meet in place of journal writing or concurrently. Check in with your partners and converse about each part of your teaching day. What were your actions? How did it go? How did you feel? Do not hash over solutions to any problems you encountered; simply note the problems and the actions you took. Do not defend or applaud your actions; this time is not for nurturing and support. It is the time for noting details, paying attention, taking notes, and consequently finding patterns. Your support group is acting merely as a sounding board, not a brainstorming mechanism. If your support group struggles with good listening, if your partners cannot withhold their advice, you may need to remind them that you are not seeking advice at this time.

Part 2: Develop a Plan

Video- or Audiotaping

Video- or audiotape your lessons. Place the camera or recorder in a discrete location, or put it on a tripod and tell your class that it is to evaluate you. You may want to vary the angles from which you shoot. Sometimes aim it where you lecture, other times try to capture the expressions and activities of your students. Watch the tape at the end of the day, alone or with your support group. Take notes on what you see, using the questions in the previous sections as guidelines.

Many presenters and teachers find video- or audiotaping a discomfiting idea. "Yikes! You mean actually tape myself so I can see every strange habit, hear every stuttered word? What? Are you kidding?" You are not required to tape, but it is the most useful tool for self-observation. Think of coaches who tape games, then review them, play-by-play, with the athletes. It might be uncomfortable to review your slip-ups, but it is a sure way to clearly and objectively see areas that you need to improve.

▶ *Exercise 2:*
Imagination Observation

Observation to discover is intended to get you comfortable during the observation process and to increase your self-awareness as you proceed through your day. It is also meant to offer clarity and understanding of how you are doing without bias toward what you think you ought to be doing. Imagination observation leads you to re-create your teaching after it has occurred.

How do you think people presently experience your teaching? Get comfortable in a sitting position. Take two or three deep cleansing breaths. Close your eyes and daydream. Use your mind's eye. Put yourself in the shoes of your students.

Envision your most recent day of teaching. Imagine yourself sitting on the receiving end of your lessons, working on the assignments, participating in student discussions and activities. Be sure in your mind that you are a student sitting in your class watching and listening to you teach. Do not re-create the scene from your familiar teacher vantage point.

If this technique works for you, remember one of your great days in class, then remember one of your worst. What was each like for you as a student? Do you get any insights as to your strengths and weaknesses as a teacher? Is their anything sweetly surprising about your teaching style? How about mortifying? This exercise can be particularly effective if you do it at the end of a teaching day and you review that entire day in your mind's eye.

Extend this visualization by imagining Albert Einstein, Cesar Chavez, Martha Graham, Igor Stravinsky, Pablo Picasso, and Mother Teresa are all children in your classroom. They have not yet become recognized for their artistic and leadership contributions to society. How do they respond to the different facets of your teaching? Imagining recognized geniuses in your class may help you realize some of the special qualities and needs of the students that you have now. Remember that right now, in someone's classroom, sits a future president of the United States. Let's hope she is learning something.

▶ *Exercise 3:*
The Survey

A third form of observation is to survey those in the know. Ask for some help, from a student, a peer, your principal, whomever might have a taste of how you are as a teacher. You might ask a number of people to get a cross-section of thoughts about your teaching. Ask them a few specific questions. You are looking for their general impressions of you as a teacher. The following questions do not cover every aspect of teaching, but should mirror for you some clear general ideas about your current style and approach as a teacher. Feel free to redesign the language of the questions to suit your class population or to uncover other information of special interest to you.

- What do you think I bring to teaching? That is, what are my special gifts, styles, or techniques as a teacher?
- What general feelings about my classes do students have? About me as a teacher? About the subject matter? About learning?
- What are my strongest ways of communicating information?
- What are two or more ways I give feedback?
- What does it feel like in my classroom? Look like? Sound like?
- How (when, what kind, what method) do I ask questions? How do I accept responses?
- What are my students doing and thinking while in my class?
- In what ways do students learn while in my class?

▶ *Exercise 4:*
Observation to Change

Observation to change asks you to look for specific things about your teaching. You can use the same techniques you used in observation to discover. Don't leave out the possibility of using friends, family, and parents of your students. Sometimes someone outside the teaching profession can offer clear and unusual insight. The main goal in this form of observation is to get greater detail about specific practices and teaching behaviors. You will use this form of observation again and again to check yourself, reformulate goals, and track progress on specific teaching goals.

Part 2: Develop a Plan

> **The more you share with others, the greater commitment and enjoyment you will experience on your professional growth journey.**

Identify the goal of your observation. Perhaps in your observation to discover you noticed some trends or habits and you want to understand why you do them. Perhaps you felt you had seen certain strengths and weaknesses and you wanted to verify your own perception of your teaching techniques. Or perhaps you have a specific lesson format that you wish to follow and you want to judge whether you are successful using that particular format. Whatever your intention, you can use observation to change to get a closer, objective look at how you are doing in the classroom. It is similar to a review by a principal, only what is being observed is more specific and teacher designed.

Move on to gathering the information. If, for instance, you want to know if you are following your lesson format in a clear manner, without backtracking or causing confusion, you first must write down the format you are using. Then you may watch your video of a typical lesson and mark on your outline whether each transition is clear to you and your students (observe their facial and verbal responses). Or you may choose to ask a student, a colleague, or an administrator to observe and mark on the outline how you handled each transition (you could ask that the observer watch the video or sit in on a lesson). You may even add specific questions to the outline: How did the students react to the transition? Was there a point at which they seemed lost?

It is important to observe and comment only on the specific area under observation. Ignore any other glaring or nonglaring concerns. You will find observation to change a tremendous tool as you determine goals to improve professionally. For instance, one teacher's observation to discover made him suspect that he was asking more questions of the students in the front of the class and that he permitted the high-achieving students to take over classroom discussions. To record and determine whether his suspicion was correct, he asked a student to track participation in class discussions by making a check mark by each student's name every time that student participated in the discussion or answered a question. The recording student did this a number of times during the week. At the end of the week, the teacher had a list with tally marks that gave a clear picture of to whom he was giving the most attention during discussions. He found that he did not favor high-achieving students so much as he favored students who sat in the front and on the right side of the room.

Next, he attempted to change his behavior by changing his classroom position. He periodically walked from one end of the classroom to the other during classroom discussions. He had the same student take another tally to learn whether his solution was enough to balance his attention. His behavior change worked! Observation to change can be used both to verify teacher behavior and to evaluate a change in behavior.

Observation to change can also be used to evaluate. Use it to measure how well you perform a specific teaching skill, then use it to check your improvement. Don't forget to record the results in some fashion so that you can include them in your professional developmental portfolio (see chapter 12).

If you have trouble coming up with specific issues to observe, go back to chapter 5, "A Teaching Ideal," and use the *The Framework for Teaching* checklist (page 57) as a starting point. Actively observe each of the four domains, or pick out specific practices within each domain. Or consider using your district's evaluation checklist as an observation to change framework.

Remember in both the discovery and change observations to get someone to help you occasionally. The more you share with others, the greater commitment and enjoyment you will experience on your professional growth journey. Consider sharing your self-observation activities in one of the following ways:

trading with a peer (you watch one teacher, then that teacher watches you)

meeting with your partner or support group

getting help from a mentor teacher

sharing your video with a nonteaching friend

checking to see if your principal will use a specific checklist during one of her classroom visits

asking a student to check off a list or answer a survey about your practices

showing a family member your video and giving them a checklist to fill out

asking a parent of a student to use a stopwatch to time your classroom transitions

▶ *Exercíse 5:*
Analysis

After you have observed yourself (with and without help) for a minimum of two weeks, hash through what you have learned. Answer at least the following questions:

1. How are you upholding your basic teacher creed, manifesto, pledge, or promise?
2. In what ways are you keeping your fundamental teaching principles in mind?

3. What teaching behaviors do you need to urgently address?
4. Do you have any bad habits?
5. In what ways do you manage your time and paperwork?
6. What ideas for change do you have that could make a powerful, positive, immediate impact?
7. Which changes could you begin tomorrow? Within the week? Within a month? Or how about within this school year?

Given the teaching behaviors that you would like to change, think about the following:

- What, if any, "hidden rewards" did you notice? For instance, do you tend to overlecture, making the teacher portion of the classroom activity too long for productive learning? If so, is the hidden reward a quiet classroom? Or the undivided attention of your students? Or do you have a habit of complaining with other teachers in the staff lounge? Perhaps the hidden reward is a sense of belonging, being part of the crowd.
- What happened directly prior to or immediately after the behavior you want to change? Sometimes what happens prior to the behavior is easier to change than the behavior. Sometimes what happens directly after the behavior is the "hidden reward."

Assignments

If you uncovered a few things from discover and imagination observation, congratulations! Reuse these observation techniques and the change observations as means to assess your skills and mark your progress in any teaching area. If you have a particular skill you want to address, but you cannot think of a way to observe and measure the skill, talk to your support group. Your partners will be a huge resource when it comes to designing creative ways to measure and assess your teaching. Brainstorm methods together.

Chapter 11 offers additional ways to track improvement, but do not neglect observation methods. The only accurate way to fully judge a softball player is to see her on the field in a ball game. Her batting average gives you some insight, and her catching and throwing or running skills may impress you, but it is the outcome of the game that counts. Likewise, the only accurate way to judge teachers is to see them in the classroom, teaching students. Use observation methods regularly; they are a valuable tool in your professional development tool kit.

I Begged Some Answer of the Night

It did me no good to ask
The night was heavy with unrest
The trees stood silent
and dared not whisper

I saw a falling star
I heard the coyote call
Only my candle flame danced

Give me a rule to follow
a discipline to heed
I begged the night

I listened
I waited
I saw

as the street lights gave in
to the night only a moth lost its way
Tomorrow's another day

—Kathleen Gumm

8

The Habits of a Teacher

It has been my experience that folks who have no vices have very few virtues.

—Abraham Lincoln

Let's all raise our hands if we have been on the self-change bandwagon before. How many of us have been successful? Not too many, I predict. I do have one friend who decides to change things and bingo, the next day he is different. I believe he is one of a kind, or one of a very few. Habits will probably be found to be connected to some sort of brain chemistry that seals them into our behavior forevermore.

This chapter is not about miracle cures and changes. If I had the answers I would not be so committed to my caffeine in the morning and chocolate in the afternoon. I have watched nail biters spend years breaking the habit only to pick it up again in a moment of crisis. My parents went through nightmares to break the habit of smoking. Some habits are promoted by addiction. Others seem to be promoted by some invisible addiction that we haven't identified yet.

Let's talk specifically about teacher habits, the little things we teachers do repeatedly that either help or hurt our teaching efforts. Sometimes little changes create a domino effect and lead to big effects. Changing the way you structure your day or instituting a ritual that leads to positive outcomes can cause a string of positive changes to happen naturally. Stopping a negative behavior can lead to enormous

> **Routine behaviors may detract from or accentuate your ability to meet your goals.**

benefits. When you change any small behavior you are bound to notice repercussions down the road. This chapter is devoted to the little changes that may make your professional growth journey enjoyable and successful.

Our brains are naturally ritualistic. We have mechanisms in place that cause us to repeat almost unconscious behaviors. You may find, for example, that you always greet your friends with the same "high five" or a specific vocalization of "Good Morning!" You may have a compulsion to brush your teeth before you shower, or check your e-mail right before you sign off the computer. These routine behaviors may detract from or accentuate your ability to meet your goals.

Understanding that we are innately habitual allows us to recognize the need for positive outlets for that ritualistic behavior. Otherwise we may find ourselves creating negative habits that undermine our goals and aspirations. In teaching, a negative ritual might be a morning routine of stopping in the teachers lounge and complaining with other teachers about everything that is wrong with the school or the students or the principal. A positive ritual might be to drop a small thank-you note in someone's box (the office manager, the crossing guard, your PTA, or another teacher) every Monday morning. A negative habit might be

Part 2: Develop a Plan

quickly turning down any school leadership position that becomes available, or just as quickly volunteering. A positive habit might be postponing your response so that you have time to decide what makes sense and meets your goals. Good habits come about when we have great mentors or instincts about rituals that are helpful. Bad teaching habits vary from teacher to teacher, school to school. Some are a result of never having put in place a good habit; some are a result of the school culture within which you work.

▶ *Exercise 1:*
Rituals and Habits

If you have carried out the observation exercises from the previous chapter, you may already have a grasp on some of the daily or weekly habits that plague or help your teaching. If you have not yet done the observation to discover or if you did not uncover any habits, rethink your day or week now. List the things that you do regularly. Do you greet your students at the door? Eat in the staff lounge? Walk around at recess? Review your plan book in the morning? Grade papers at the end of the day? Overschedule your day? Rush the end of lessons? Allow papers to pile up? Say "yes" or "no" to requests without thinking them through? List as many rituals and habits as you can. Put stars next to any that you think compliment your overall success as a teacher.

As you go through the following exercises, return to your list as a source of information about what you do and don't do. I will focus on bad and good habits that I know about, but I encourage you to relate your own personal experiences to the rituals I suggest.

▶ *Exercise 2:*
Changing Bad Habits

Look over the discoveries from chapter 7 or this chapter and choose a habit you would like to be rid of. Then choose one of the following approaches and work on changing the habit. Evaluate your progress every two weeks in your journal or with your support group.

Replace

It is often easier to replace a negative habit with a positive habit, such as replacing smoking with gum chewing, than to extinguish the habit completely. In fact, for some of us this is the only possible method for change. When you notice you have a bad habit, deliberately choose a good habit to develop in place of it. Each time you catch yourself in the midst of the bad habit, replace it with the good.

Observe and Understand

Observing the patterns that lead to the habit can help you get rid of it. Observe yourself. What happens right before you behave in the habitual way? Right after? Is the habit associated with some other activity? My parents had to give up bowling in order to give up smoking! Talk with your support group and write in your journal about the habit you are trying to extinguish. Ask why you do it and when you do it. Brainstorm every possible reason you cannot stop this habit. Include even the silliest possibilities that lead you to engage in this habit. What are the reinforcers (the unseen rewards) you may be getting? They may be random, that is, you may not get the rewards every time you engage in the habit, but you get them enough to make the habit worth keeping to you. What feelings are associated with the habit? That is, do you do it when you feel frustrated or tired? Such observation of your habit may help you find a path to correcting the problem. Look for patterns to disrupt. We teach impulsive children to recognize emotional signals before the impulsive behavior. What signals can you note and deal with up front to bring about a different behavior? Is there some way to remind yourself in advance and to change the precursor to the habit?

> **Look for patterns to disrupt.**

Reminders

Some of us need reminders that we have started a new habit or are fighting an old one. Do something to remind yourself that you are trying to change. Put your reminder in a place where you are likely to see it at the moment the habitual impulse is likely to hit. If you are an overlecturer, for example, you might put a notice on your podium or in the back of your room that says, "Those who are doing all the talking are doing all the learning." Be sure not to take on more than one or two new habits at a time. Otherwise your reminder list will be huge and you will stop looking at it.

Seeking Help

If your habit is very disruptive and difficult to change, I suggest seeking extra help. Having the consciousness and conscientiousness to know you need to fix something is 90 percent of the battle. There is no shame in asking for help and ideas from friends, your support group, your principal or students, or even a professional counselor. They may have creative methods for helping to intervene.

Part 2: Develop a Plan

▶ *Exercise 3:*
Creating Good Habits

Choose something that you think is missing from your lists. What habit do you value as a teacher that you are not currently practicing? Choose from the following methods to begin instilling the new habit.

Create Reinforcements

Rewards and punishments have been shown to actually decrease motivation, so when I use the term *reinforcements*, I use it warily. The best reinforcement comes from a strong inner motivation to change; otherwise, you will actually undermine your own efforts. I recommend reinforcement that is cerebral, such as a quiet moment to notice that you succeeded, rather than material, such as a new car. You may arrange your calendar so that an activity you look forward to immediately follows a behavior that you wish to encourage. If you hate organizing your desk, organize it before you leave each day, then take that walk in the park you love. The next morning be sure to take note of your clean desk and your feelings of success.

Cues and Associations

To embark on establishing a good habit, it is often useful to associate the habit with a "cue," an established routine. For instance, when I wanted to start my family on a vitamin supplement, I had to tie it into one of our daily routines—brushing our teeth. I know people who exercise during a favorite TV program and others who walk immediately upon waking in the morning. You may have to try different options to see which works best (before reading the newspaper, during snack time, before turning the TV on after school, and so on), but the trick is to keep to the new routine faithfully for a period of a few weeks. After that it will become part of the previous routine, and you will do it almost automatically.

> *The best reinforcement comes from a strong inner motivation to change.*

Some General Guidelines

1. AVOID SELF-BEATINGS AND "NOW-I-BLEW-IT" THINKING

If you manage to get started on a habit, then forget or become stressed and stop, don't count all as lost. Change your perception about delays and setbacks. They are merely short rest stops on your journey. If you call them rest stops, then the "genuine" you always comes back to the habit. If you call them failures, then your self-perception is that you do not already have these habits as part of your lifestyle. "I blew my diet. Oh, well, I guess I'll eat like a pig" versus "I can get back to eating properly."

Let's say for some reason you stopped brushing your teeth for a day or two; you got busy or forgot your toothbrush on a trip. My guess is you would say "oops," then get right back to regularly brushing your teeth. You would not say, "Oh, well, guess I just cannot acquire that habit. I might as well give up." Think of habits as lifestyle changes that you have already made. There is no option to quit. Neglecting the habit is an error to correct, not proof of failure.

2. WHAT HAS WORKED BEFORE?

Do you currently have a good habit or ritual that you practice faithfully? Or is there an old bad habit that you managed to quit? If you can think back and replay in your mind the method you used to change those habits successfully, then you have a promising method to try out for other changes.

Some Typical Teacher Habits

Following are explanations of and possible solutions to several teacher habits I have noticed. The list is by no means exhaustive, but it can be useful in many ways. You may see a habit in the descriptions you would like to change, particularly if you are having difficulty coming up with one. They may also spark an associative idea that you would like to work on. Finally, they show the habit changing process when it's applied to genuine problems.

Staff Lounge Gossip

We all can find comfort in sharing our challenges as teachers. Such behavior can make us feel as though we're "one of the gang." But we can develop the habit of spending break periods with other staff members bemoaning or gossiping about the school, the students, the administration, the parents, the community, and anything else we can think of. While this behavior may be the result of some very real problems in a district or school, it brings down self-motivation as well as the motivation of anyone else present. It also depresses morale.

I suggest replacing this habit with something positive that gives you a sense of belonging. Start your own teacher support group. Or continue to meet teachers in the lounge, but make a point of replacing the negative pronouncements with something positive. Ask about families and vacations. Ask about lessons that gave them particular success. Make a point of giving genuine compliments on a daily basis. Your change in attitude will help extinguish your bad habit and may even affect the attitudes of others.

Negative Self-Talk

We all can allow our mind's voice to criticize every unsuccessful lesson or classroom slip-up, recalling every mistake made just to confirm our own incompetence. This behavior does nothing to help us improve and generally detracts from our true successes. Often these messages are hybrids of what we might have heard growing up: "You idiot! What's the matter with you? Can't you get anything right?"

Replace your negative messages with self-affirmations. A self-affirmation is a statement you repeat aloud or in your mind that encourages and promotes your positive attributes. Use an affirmation as a way to rule out the other voices in your head. Pick something specific you want to work on and say it every night, such as "I can be a patient listener" or "I know how to enjoy life." When you do something well, say to yourself, "Hey, good job." When you complete a difficult project, say to yourself, "I stuck with it! I am persistent." When you acquire a new habit, say "I am capable of changing!" Use positive moments as a way of turning around any negative voices in your head. If you make a mistake and you hear your inner critic, respond with "Mistakes are part of learning."

I doubted the usefulness of affirmations until I experienced their success in a child I know. A friend had taken to sitting every night with his fearful, anxious, nervous six-year-old and having her repeat the words, "I am not afraid to experience life!" One evening about four months after he had begun this ritual, this same little girl was the first of ten children to attempt a flip right off the diving board. Shortly thereafter she auditioned for the school talent show and raced the other children to the water slides at a local theme park. Her fears of the world were definitely diminished. Certainly this one example is not proof that affirmations work in every situation, but it gave me plenty to think about.

Blaming the World

It's tempting to escape to the comfort of blaming other people. "The lesson wasn't successful because the students are rude." "My students aren't successful because their parents don't help." "If we didn't have this standardized test looming, I could really teach these students something."

The "Serenity Prayer" comes in useful here: "Grant me the serenity to accept the things I cannot change, the courage to change the things I can, and the wisdom to know the difference." Replace the blame habit with something more positive. When you feel the blame-monster rise up, think of at least three ways you can personally affect the situation: "Well, I could donate time or money to a worthy agency that helps with this problem." "I could try changing my approach and see if I get better results." "I could volunteer to lead up that committee and make the needed changes happen." If you can't come up with any, then let it go.

I am not candy-coating situations. Most volunteers I know all agree that their blaming began to disintegrate the moment they began to put energy into the problem. One volunteer I spoke with told me, "I kept thinking, why doesn't somebody do something? Then I realized I am somebody." Proactive behavior helps us to feel empowered and capable and, in some situations, more compassionate.

If I Don't Do It, Nobody Will

Ah, the "I can't say no" syndrome. Saying "yes" to all requests. Teachers can be martyrs; we say "yes," then complain that we are overloaded. Probably the career attracts caring, helping people who love to be needed and wanted, which means we tend to overcommit until we burn out. If we continuously accept and take on new responsibilities without ever letting go of some of the old, we will reach a critical point where our attitudes change. Certainly, turning into negative, overwhelmed complainers is not our ultimate goal.

Learn to select carefully and know what you are going to give up each time you take on something new. Practice a new habit: when someone asks you to join or to help or to do, stop yourself from jumping in. Thank them for the opportunity and say you will think about it. This response is not an automatic rejection; it is a delay so that you can make wise, thought-through choices. Then take your time figuring out whether this request is something you want to fulfill.

I was asked to take over the treasury of my local PTA. As anyone knows the treasury is a big job, but the previous treasurer quit rather suddenly, and since I am familiar with accounting, people thought of me. I delayed my response and thought about it. I decided that I enjoy numbers and I wouldn't mind doing that part of the job, but I hate evening meetings and I did not want to take care of deposits. I offered to take on only the part with which I felt comfortable, and the PTA board quickly found people willing to take over the other portions of the job. Because I thought through the request, I did not take on too much and never felt put upon.

If I Don't Do It, Somebody Else Will

Here we have the "I can't say yes" syndrome. Saying "no" automatically whenever you are asked for extra help will also tear away at your self-esteem because it generally is an overreaction to the above syndrome or a fear of being swallowed whole. I hear so many people say, "Oh, I would volunteer also, but I know then I just won't be able to break away." Instead they sit on the sidelines, wishing more could be done and wondering "why somebody doesn't do it."

Again I recommend the "hesitate before you answer" approach. You can always say "no." Hesitating and giving yourself some time to think may give you

Part 2: Develop a Plan

the inspiration to chip in once in a while and try out your leadership wings. Get into the habit of stopping when someone makes a request and listening closely to the request. Then let them know you will think about it. Perhaps you will find you would enjoy and feel fulfilled from the work they are proposing.

Pileup

Teachers with this habit should not feel alone. Paperwork and other lackluster duties can become overwhelming when you teach. The more subjects or classes you teach, the more miscellaneous duties you have to deal with. For some of us, the paperwork is the least interesting part of the job and it is easy to put it aside. Often, we respond to these assignments by avoiding them, but such a habit can result in a domino effect of secondary problems. Our students don't receive immediate feedback on their work, which results in slower learning. Our principals become irritated with our inconsistent organization, which results in workplace tension.

> **Give something new and different a chance occasionally.**

Visit a local bookstore in the home office management section; note the sheer number of best-selling books on organizing and managing your office (your home, your life). Such numbers tell us we are not the only ones who suffer from this habit. Organizing paperwork can be complex and requires forethought on your part. You have to determine where all the papers are coming from. Are they papers for correcting? Papers for filing? Work sheets? Memos and information from the office? Lesson planning materials? Papers to correct?

Before developing any systems, find a teacher who is successful at managing papers. Ask that teacher how she tracks and organizes each type of paperwork. Set up files, boxes, or shelves with sections for each type so you can keep the different types separated. Then look at each type of paper as an individual issue to address. Perhaps memos from the office can be handled immediately when you receive them, and lesson planning materials can always be put away at the beginning of the week. Are you collecting more papers from your students than you need to collect? If you are just collecting in order to correct, perhaps you can develop a classroom system for correcting certain types of papers. Assign students or volunteers to do the correcting. If you feel the amount you are collecting is what you actually must collect, then begin to associate paper correcting with a cue. When the bell rings, for example, the paper correcting begins. When paper correcting is complete, then you can visit the staff lounge. Develop a habit for doing it right away and it will not become part of the pileup problem.

Phone Call Avoidance

It isn't fun to call parents if your news is less than stellar, which is why we might tend to put off calling. We ignore the behavior problem or give consequences repeatedly without ever calling home to discuss the issue with parents. We wait until report card time to give a full picture to parents. Bad habit. The consequences can be severe. Parents will complain that you gave them no opportunity to help you help their child—and they are right. Parents may spread negative reports about you among themselves.

Two possible solutions to this problem: One, call parents at the beginning of the year with a nice anecdote about their child and school. They will have a positive first impression that can do wonders if the time comes that you have to call with less happy thoughts. Two, whenever you do need to make that negative phone call home, follow up immediately with a positive call to a different students' parents. That way the anxiety of the first call can be somewhat alleviated.

Getting into a Teaching Rut

We've all been in a rut that frustrated and bored us. Are you locked in to using the same exact lesson format for every lesson? Does your classroom period have the same beginning, middle, and end as it has for 25 years?

The first trick to beating this bad habit is to change something. Change anything. Change the way you start each lesson. Change where you stand or how you look. Take a class at the local college in some subject you have never studied and learn from the instructor at least three new ways to teach new material. Our local city manager has a favorite quotation: "When something isn't broken, break it." The quotation is intended to avoid the lack of change that breeds complacency. What worked for you before may still be working, but try something new for the sheer excitement of it. You are a human being; you are built to break the mold once in a while. You can always return to your old structure and format, but give something new and different a chance occasionally. You may reinvigorate your teaching and your students' learning.

Good Habits to Foster

The following are habits that you will want to foster even if you have no corresponding bad habit to replace.

Affirmations

We spoke before of changing negative self-talk. Your teacher manifesto or some simple affirmative statements can be just the ticket to overcoming negative self-talk, but they are valuable as regular rituals as well. Before class every morning, review your manifesto or a series of positive affirmations. "Learning is exciting for me and my students." "My classroom is a welcoming, safe place to learn." "I am interested and therefore interesting."

Autonomy

Autonomy is really an outlook on life, and it is an essential ingredient to personal success and motivation. You can encourage and invite your own teaching autonomy by making a personal choice every day. Instead of going through your entire day teaching prearranged lessons from prearranged formats, add something of you. Tell a joke, draw a picture, grow plants, incorporate something of yourself into the learning approach or environment. You will begin to develop a stronger sense of your independent teaching self and your students will benefit by your modeling.

Complainathon

I would love to claim this concept as my original idea, but it comes from Barbara Sher (1979), author of *Wishcraft: How to Get What You Really Want*. Sher recommends vigorous griping as a way to overcome complacency, and I agree. Try it on pa-

> **Do all of it big. Really big.**

per or with a cheerleading friend. You can institute this practice at the beginning of each support group meeting. The idea is to blame everyone. Scream aloud. Call yourself names. Make excuses. But do all of it big. Really big. Complain and gripe and groan and blow everything hugely out of proportion until you feel resolved. It is like taking all of your negative packaging and blowing it up until it becomes silly. Give it a try; you will be amazed how gratifying and satisfying and even motivating it is to just cut loose with no judgment hanging over your head. The difference between this approach and the blaming and griping I list under teacher bad habits is that this is done in a specific format. You, and anyone else participating, know your true aim is to blow off steam until you are out of steam. It is not about a continuous slow whine that drags you down, but rather a large freeing explosion.

Spend Time with an Energizer or a Stress Reducer

Who or what energizes or relaxes you? If you are energized or relaxed, the benefits are enormous to your teaching. I suggest you make visits with that individual or activity regularly.

A Challenge

Do all of these behaviors sound foreign? You may not relate to any of these habits. You may have other behaviors you would like to extinguish or encourage. Use any of the methods I listed at the beginning of this chapter, or design a method all your own. The foremost necessity to bringing about change, clichéd as it sounds, is to really want to change. If the desire truly comes from within, the chances of successfully changing are very good whatever method you use.

Small Things

The small moments
small topics on
weekends and the weather
Small ideas, empty places
paper wads, the vacant spaces
Spring planters filled with nothing
but daisies

Small rooms of time
that children are small children
Lime and green
and growing up.

—Kathleen Gumm

9

The Growth of a Teacher

Everyone thinks of changing the world, but no one thinks of changing himself.

—Leo Tolstoy

Are you thinking: "Here it comes, 'the plan.' All I need is yet another 'plan' to bury me in details and ruin any fun there is to teaching." Relax. The next step is not a lifetime plan with step-by-step objectives that will control your every teaching moment. Nor do I condone a laissez-faire, let-it-all-land-where-it-lands approach to professional growth. As you proceed through the next three chapters, you will learn a method for professional growth that is neither too contrived, nor too lacking in direction. The method I advocate will allow you to reach for your highest aspirations without being buried in details on a daily basis.

Keep in mind that, as a teacher, your professional growth is a lifetime project. There is no rush to complete everything this week. In fact it is crucial that you take your time working toward your ideals; otherwise you might burn out before you even get to see any results. Break it all down. Take very small steps, and before you know it you will have completed one project and be moving on to the next.

For some of you anything I suggest about professional growth will be old news. Many schools and districts have very complete professional growth planning packages that will help you easily break your ideals into individual goals and map out plans from year to year. Use your district's ideas and plans. They may be tied to your district and administration priorities, but usually they will be broad enough to accommodate any of your personal aspirations as a teacher, as well. Teachers and their supervisors have been known to fill in these plans after the work has been done (spoken by a teacher who has been guilty of this misdemeanor). In those first few years, doing anything but teaching the basics seems impossible. But you will truly benefit and feel good about your progress if you draw up the plans first and fill in your accomplishments after you have reached your goals. It will help you in so many ways.

> **Teaching is a broad career. There are continuous opportunities for learning.**

Teaching is a broad career; there are continuous opportunities for learning. If every single workshop or conference or staff development seems applicable... it is. But you cannot spend all your time running around to every single training offered or reading every single book published. Instead, select your goal priorities, then hone the list of what you are looking for. You will increase your time learning and mastering any particular areas of interest before moving on to the next area of interest. You will be designing your own professional development curriculum.

Part 2: Develop a Plan

After the first session in a twelve-week parenting course, one of the participants called me at home. She explained that she was very excited about setting some house rules and living by them. She had followed the class outline and developed some basic rules, but now she was having problems posting them on her refrigerator; there was not enough room. Did I have another idea about where she might fit all of the new rules?

"All of the new rules?" I questioned.

"Yes," she said, "I settled on twenty-five to start!"

It must be human nature that we tend to overdo the rules and goals. I assured her that while her ambition was impressive, a smaller list of fewer than five rules would be easier to remember and therefore more effective. The same goes for professional growth planning. You may want to do it all! Over time you might even be able to accomplish it all. But to begin, it is best to make your list of goals and rules short. This chapter is intended to help you make the list short and easy to handle.

Begin by gathering the various lists and ideas you have been acquiring by doing the exercises from the beginning of this book.

▶ *Exercise 1:*
Reading through Your Lists

Start by finding one spot to keep all of the ideas and lists. The spot can be at school or at home, in a box or a file cabinet. You don't need to sort or label the lists and ideas; just throw them together in one place where you can easily find them when you need them. If you are a stickler for staying tidy and organized, file the lists by the chapters in this book (heart discoveries, mind discoveries, soul discoveries, ideals, self-observations, and habits), or you might create your own categories. Or you can subdivide by professional growth areas identified by your school or district. However, for the purposes of planning, you need only to find one spot to store these lists.

> *To begin, . . . make your list of goals and rules short.*

Take two reading excursions. The first excursion is a reading jaunt through your journal. You probably have a large number of entries by this time and you may already have done some reading through your morning pages. As you read through the pages, jot down on index cards ideas for professional development that may show up in the pages. Put each idea on a separate index card to facilitate grouping and sorting.

Ideas in your journal will show up in one of two ways. You may notice a recurring theme or frustration that needs to be addressed; perhaps you are consistently complaining about feeling unprepared for your lessons or frustrated by lack of student interest. You may get sudden inspirations right in the middle of your pages, some theme unit you would like to design or a new system to organize paper collection. If you have not kept a journal, but you have been attending a teacher support group, work with your group to write up a host of index cards with goals you would like to accomplish or problems you would like to address.

The second reading jaunt is through all of the notes you have acquired. Review the notes from the heart, mind, and soul chapters. Review your notes from the ideal teacher chapter and your passive and active self-observations. Finally, review any notes you may have taken regarding teacher habits. In one sitting look through all of these various lists and pay attention to recurring themes and ideas that hold your interest or excite you. Put these ideas or goals onto individual index cards as well.

▶ *Exercise 2:*
Grouping and Sorting

Take all the cards you have and spread them out on the floor. Group them by similarities, like a cluster graph. One group might have cards that list paperwork issues, lesson plan issues, and other issues related to teacher organization. Another group of cards might list learning about brain research, reading a book on accelerated learning techniques, and other issues related to keeping current. If one goal is to create a system for paperwork and one is to grade papers daily, they belong together. If one card mentions learning about brain research and another goal is to read a book on accelerated ways of learning, put those cards together. If you have a number of cards relating to developing better relationships with colleagues or improving rapport with your students, put those cards together. Continue sorting until all your cards are in groups.

If you struggle with how to formulate your groups you can use the four domains from the *The Framework for Teaching* list (page 57) in "A Teaching Ideal" or the categories offered by your school district. My district offers the following categories:

teacher strategies and procedures
classroom management
professional responsibilities

Look at each group of cards separately. If you have five cards in one group, decide which card in that group has greatest priority based on your own sense of urgency. Place that card on top of that pile, then paper-clip the cards together.

Exercise 3:
A Short List

List the top priorities (the top card from each pile). Add any other items that did not make the top of their group but intrigue you anyway. If you feel you would be highly motivated to accomplish some item that did not make the "urgent" list, add that item, as well. Some of the items you list may be quick improvements that you wish to make within your classroom or in your teaching. Other items might be long-term goals you hope to accomplish over the years. Some items might be projects, things that you make or create and then they are finished. In that case, check them off; you don't return to that particular goal or step. Other goals might be processes that involve improving some aspect of your teaching or concentrating on some relationship that you have neglected, such as getting to know students better or reaching out to other teachers. These kinds of improvements are never really finished but rather something that you work on all of the time.

On a new sheet, make the heading "Projects." On this sheet, list appropriate items from your short list. They might include the following:

Develop a theme unit on "Inventions."

Read The First Days of School *to get ideas for classroom setup.*

Complete a class on teaching reading.

Rearrange my desk.

Develop a paper management system.

Put together the materials for a notebook journal.

Now make another sheet titled "Processes" that includes projects such as the following:

Get to know my students better.

Improve communication with my principal.

Improve my attitude about schools and teaching.

Learn about brain research.

Learn about learning styles and teaching styles.

Reflect on my teaching regularly.

If you find that one list has significantly more items than the other, add at least three other items to the other list. Having your entire goal list fall into one side or the other is a sign that you may not appreciate the need for balance in your professional planning. Perhaps you are one of those results-oriented individuals who has a tendency to ignore the people factors such as feelings and relationships. Perhaps you are a process-oriented individual who tends to lean so much to feelings and relationships, or who enjoys "stopping to smell the flowers," that occasionally you need that little push of a deadline. In addition, be sure there is at least one project on that list that you can accomplish in fewer than two weeks.

Once you have two lists of at least seven items but no more than, say, ten each, you are almost ready for "Getting Started." However, first we need to brainstorm and plan some details for at least a few of the items. Put your index cards and all your lists into your storage file or box. You will not look at all these papers again until you have completed some of your goals and are looking for new projects or processes. Keep out only your project and process lists.

▶ *Exercise 4:*
Choose the Goal

Pick from your lists one of the more complex project items and one of the more complex process items. By *complex* I mean goals that will take more than one or two weeks and one or two steps to accomplish. Pick each based on your gut reaction. If it feels like a project or process you really want to get started on, then move that one to the front of the pack.

If you find yourself struggling when trying to pick from so many possible goals, try these ideas:

- Choose the shortest, easiest goal to give yourself a shot in the arm. Find the one that will have the biggest effect with the least amount of work.
- Choose the goal that you keep looking at and thinking about. If it easily pops to the forefront of your mind even when you are not looking at lists, it holds some fascination for you.
- Choose the goal that you feel has the most easily determined steps.
- Choose the goal with which someone near you can help. If you have a teacher on staff who is a master in one area and you have a goal to improve in that area, choose that goal.

▶ *Exercise 5:*
Map Out a Project Plan

Look at the project item. On a blank sheet of paper put the result of the project on the right side of your page and circle it. For instance, if the project is to develop a new theme unit, put down "new theme unit" and circle it. Then, starting on the left side of your page, write things you will need to accomplish to

Part 2: Develop a Plan

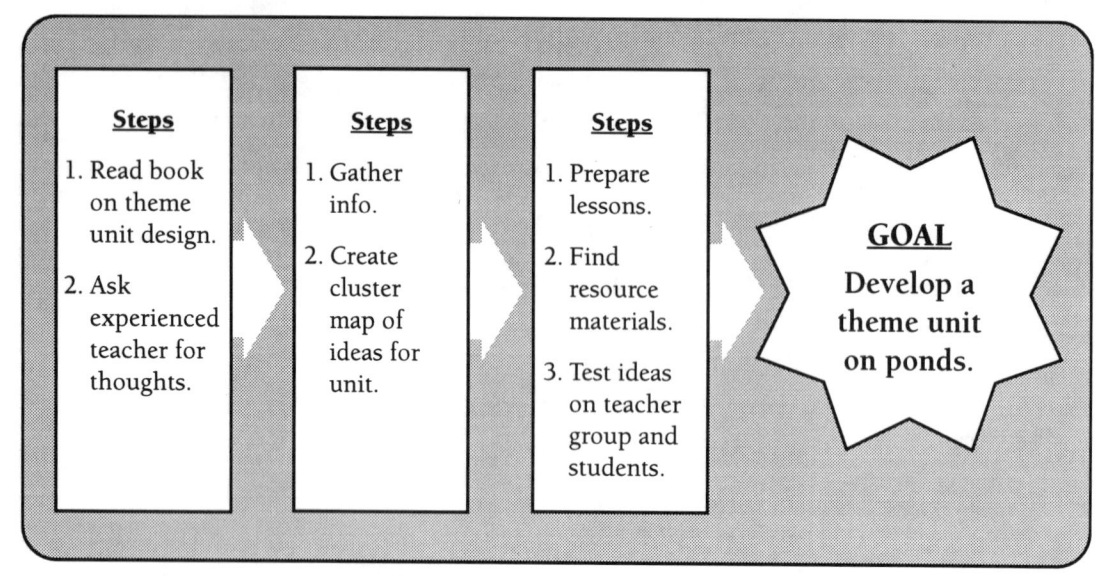

Steps	Steps	Steps	
1. Read book on theme unit design.	1. Gather info.	1. Prepare lessons.	**GOAL**
2. Ask experienced teacher for thoughts.	2. Create cluster map of ideas for unit.	2. Find resource materials.	Develop a theme unit on ponds.
		3. Test ideas on teacher group and students.	

Figure 1. Web of project plan

reach your goal. Work slowly to your right until you reach the circled product (see figure 1).

You can also start just to the left of the project and plan backward. For instance, you may write, "teach the unit" and "evaluate the unit." To the left of those thoughts you might write "create a chart of theme-related ideas for various subject areas" and "design the unit." To the left of those ideas you might write "pick a theme to use" and "talk to teachers who have done theme units." Finally, all the way to the left, "Read Susan Kovalik's book on theme units."

Perhaps you will need to investigate a great deal before you actually plan out the project. Write down all possible avenues for investigation on the left side and leave the rest of the page blank for future planning.

▶ *Exercise 6:*

Map Out a Process Plan

Look at the process item. Write the concept in the center of a blank sheet of paper and circle it. Brainstorm ideas that will help you improve, affect, work on, and influence the process you have written down. For instance, if the process you have chosen is to improve student motivation, write that in the middle of your page. Then begin to come up with places you should look, things you should learn, people you should talk to, ideas you might have, all leading to the goal of improving student motivation. Perhaps you know of a good book on motivation techniques; write "read the book," then add a second step, "try out ideas," on the

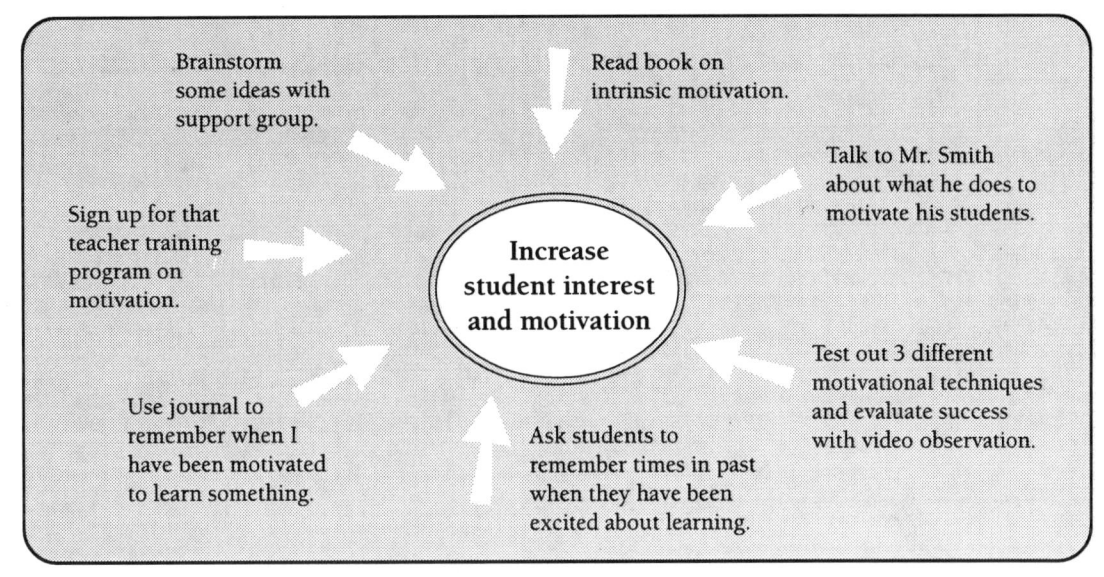

```
                    Read book on
Brainstorm          intrinsic motivation.
some ideas with
support group.
                                            Talk to Mr. Smith
                                            about what he does to
Sign up for that                            motivate his students.
teacher training         Increase
program on            student interest
motivation.           and motivation
                                            Test out 3 different
                                            motivational techniques
Use journal to                              and evaluate success
remember when I      Ask students to        with video observation.
have been motivated  remember times in past
to learn something.  when they have been
                     excited about learning.
```

Figure 2. Web of process plan

way to the center concept. You can see that mapping out a process goal is different from mapping out a project goal because there is no discernible product that lets you know you are there. Instead, you just devote time to the process and evaluate your progress (see figure 2).

▶ *Exercise 7:*
Evidence of Growth

The final step before you start your steps is designing some methods for measuring your success. Any evidence of success or progress is an indicator. A good test score might be one indicator that students have learned a particular subject. One reason to develop indicators is for your own satisfaction. It is one thing to accomplish a goal; it is another thing to have proof of that accomplishment. Certificates, diplomas, trophies, and report cards all point to the satisfaction we humans receive by having indicators or evidence of our progress. Indicators also help you evaluate your accomplishment by giving you something tangible to judge.

Another reason for developing indicators is your professional portfolio. You can make your portfolio much more powerful by including proof of each successful step you take on the road to professional self-development.

Onward to "Getting Started," which is easy to do—a lot of the work is already done!

Render Me

Someone to cry to
to till the hard soil
rinse the seeds of stagnation
I find myself in, embedded deep

Some room to gather
up summer around me
where I can collect enough
petals to form a whole flower

Some fertile field
to grow into myself

—Kathleen Gumm

Part 3

Take Action

10

Getting Started and Building Momentum

The only place where success comes before work is in the dictionary.
—Vidal Sassoon

Getting Started and Building Momentum

It takes a significant push to dislodge a rock at the top of a hill; from then on gravity does the work and the rock gains momentum as it goes. Getting started on anything seems so difficult. How many would-be novelists talk about looking forward to retirement when they can finally sit down and write that novel they have been dreaming about? How many times do you hear people say, "I am going to start working out? Or eating better? Or taking a morning walk?" How often do you see all the materials for a household building project sitting unused out in a tool shed ten years later? We humans like to procrastinate.

So here I am asking you to get started on a professional growth project, a project you will never actually finish, that will take time and energy and concentration and who knows what else. Is this going to be yet another of those half-baked ideas that sits barely started in the garage? Is this going to be something else you do not finish that hangs around on your calendar making you feel bad every time you look at it?

The first thing you need to know: getting started is entirely up to you . . . groan. I know it is frustrating to realize, but all those unfinished projects are nothing more than a decision away from happening. Your decision. Your choice. Choose action. Even slow action is ever so much more interesting than nonaction.

What holds people up if it is so easy? Sometimes it is the sense of being overwhelmed and wanting life to be simpler. Sometimes it is because the desire is not really their own in the first place. They only "thought" they wanted to change; turns out it was really someone else's idea. Sometimes it is because so many projects have been left in storage that they no longer believe they are capable. Every new unfinished project just adds to the pile of a decaying esteem.

The first time many teachers consider planning their professional development is when they receive professional planning packets from their principal, district, or credential board. Such material may look like drudgery to do, but often it can fit perfectly with personal plans for professional development. Most professional packets are broad enough to fit personal priorities into the framework. People can meet their own needs while fulfilling administrative requirements.

▶ *Exercise 1:*
Professional Development Sheet

You are a teacher and no doubt your plate is always full. Yet addressing professional growth goals will, in the long run, make your job easier and more satisfying. To begin, title a sheet "Professional Development Sheet." Study your process and project maps. Pick three steps that you can accomplish quickly and that will have an immediate positive impact, and list them on the sheet. Be sure to choose

Part 3: Take Action

from project and process maps. You must be able to accomplish the steps within a week or two. Quick success ideas are great for starting your engine. Better to think to yourself, "No sweat, I can do THAT," than to put something down that you might avoid starting. These steps become your goals.

> *The key to . . . keeping yourself going lies in attitude, momentum, and proof of accomplishment.*

Never list more than three steps on your professional development sheet at one time. The long lists you made before the planning chapter belong in your file cabinet, out of sight and out of mind. The shorter list of goals and the maps you created at the end of the last chapter is what you use to choose your steps. Keep these accessible, but out of sight.

Post your three current steps somewhere that you look every day. Most teachers prefer posting them at the top of the weekly lesson plan book. If you don't use a lesson plan book, the top of your weekly calendar or a slip of paper taped to the top of your bathroom mirror may work well. When you complete a step, place it on a gold-star list of accomplishments (see motivation).

Complete all three steps before listing three more. If you finish all three quickly, within three or four days, then you can take a break for the rest of the two weeks or, if you are feeling charged and motivated, take advantage of the steam and formulate three more items to work on.

Every time you select three new goals, evaluate them. If you cannot meet them in two weeks, perhaps you can see your way to breaking them down into even smaller steps and listing those. Make sure you include the "big goal" in parentheses next to the small step; it will motivate you by keeping the small step connected to the big picture.

If you have not done the exercises in the previous chapter, you might to do this exercise differently. Perhaps you have been reading this book, but you haven't really tried any of the exercises. You are the kind of person who likes to read through it all before starting. Your first three steps might look something like this:

1. Buy a notebook and set up dividers (project goal; quick success) so I can use it as a journal.

2. Ask Amanda and/or Dan if they are interested in a support group. (process goal; form a partner or support group)

3. Jog three days so I don't go mad! (project goal; run in 10K race)

The following week your goals might look something like this:
1. Write in journal four days this week. (process goal; quick success)
2. Finish reading 3 *Cheers for Teaching.* (project goal; change habits)
3. Play 3 days this week. (process goal; attitude adjustment)

If you have been doing all the exercises chapter by chapter as you moved through this book, congratulations! You have made huge progress. You probably already meet regularly with your support group and keeping your journal is a snap. Plus you have already incorporated play into your life. You can select three goals that directly address your list of ideas from the growth planning chapter. Your first three steps might look something like this:
1. Place a big, attractive box next to my desk to gather portfolio materials. (project; quick success)
2. Talk to Jim about his classroom setup and why it works for him. Research two other possible setups from other teachers. (project goal; adjust classroom setup)
3. Try the cooperative learning lesson from the book I am reading. If I like it, think of three other lessons where I might use the same format. (process goal; use cooperative learning more often)

So that's it. You have set up your three-step method of professional growth. You have put the crowbar under the rock and begun to lift. Once you have a list of steps to meet your goal, the key to getting started and keeping yourself going lies in attitude, momentum, and proof of accomplishment. Attitude is the most important element.

▶ *Exercise 2:*
Attitude Busters

The first part of changing your attitude is being aware that it needs changing. If you have been journal writing since the beginning of this book, you may have noticed negative attitude markers popping up, such statements as "This is stupid," or "This is crazy," or "This is too difficult"; "I can't," or "I'm not capable," or "What is the matter with me?" If you have not been journal writing, ask your support group or a good friend whom you trust to be honest about your attitude. Also, listen to your inner thoughts. Are they negative and pessimistic? If you find that yes, in fact, your attitude does need some adjustment, read on.

Did you read the habits chapter? If you have not yet tried affirmations or a complainathon, give them a try now. They are terrific attitude busters. The complainathon is silly fun and will help you leapfrog over all the arguments you post against getting started. The affirmations will begin the war against all those negative critics inside your head. Turn back to those exercises now if you need a refresher.

Next, write in your journal or discuss with your group to identify an attitude that you think is keeping you from getting started on the goals you identified in the previous chapter. Then choose one or more of the following methods to guide you in changing that attitude.

Inner Dare

Occasionally, when I am wary of a new project, when I know I want to do it but I can't seem to get up the nerve, I dare myself. I talk to my insides and say, "Go for it! Do it! You chicken . . . leap!" Generally, these statements cause all those nervous tensions of childhood to return, but like when I was a child . . . I leap! It may mean getting off to a stuttery, shaky start, but at least it is a start. Such an approach really involves ignoring or overriding my attitude toward the project. To get started on my first book, I dared myself to propose my idea to a publisher, unsolicited and unplanned. I had a brief opportunity and I leapt in. Once I started the proposal, I could not go backward and unsay it. So, how can you use this technique to initiate your goals?

Look at a step on your current list and dare yourself to get started: "I dare myself to put together an example portfolio for that next staff meeting!" (Whoops, did I say that?) And there you are, off and running.

Failures and Mistakes

One important attitude characteristic is how you view failures and mistakes. If all those unfinished projects in the garage translate into self-beatings, "I am a failure," then you need to adjust the way you look at failures. Let go of the self-beating and the unfinished projects. Clean out materials that were meant for projects you never finished. Give yourself the sense that your slate is now clear. You are starting over!

If a mistake translates for you into proof you are incapable, then you must change that attitude, as well. Thomas Edison attempted to invent the lightbulb enough times to fry even the brightest brain, but he kept going. His perception was that each failed bulb brought him closer to the version that would work. You must begin to see *your* mistakes as part of *your* path. Think of ways you can fail at or make a mistake on the step you have chosen to begin. Mentally acknowledge your error with one small "oops." Then ask yourself what you can change the next time through. Replay it in your mind to practice. Remember: Perfection is dull and you are infinitely interesting.

Play

If you have been ignoring the simple joys we discussed all the way back in chapter 2, then your attitude is likely to be sour. Look at the goal you have chosen and make it into a game. How can it be playful? Fun? What can you do to make it more fun? For your general attitude, you can institute a playtime every week or you will be unable to overcome your lethargy.

Changing Your Thinking

The most effective, long-lasting attitude booster is a complete change in thinking. Yes, we can teach our minds to think more optimistically. Martin Seligman (1996), a researcher and author of the books *Learned Optimism* and *The Optimistic Child*, teaches us to ask logical, open-ended questions to reframe our thoughts about things. Once you have identified negative thinking patterns, you evaluate the accuracy of your thinking. Let's say you have a goal to start bringing humor into your classroom lessons. Your inner voice tells you this idea is stupid; you are no good at telling jokes, you don't even know if the humor research is accurate, and you have too many other things to worry about. How's that for negative thinking?

Look at the step or goal you have chosen, and ask yourself the following questions to challenge negative roadblocks:

- What is the worse thing that can happen?
- What are some of the possible consequences if the worst thing happens?
- Can I live with those consequences?
- How likely is it that the worse thing will happen?
- What is most likely to occur?
- What might I gain if this works?

When you are confronted by any challenge, use these questions to overcome your fear and pessimism. Use them with a friend or partner so that you have an extra voice to keep you from dwelling on the negative possibilities.

If you find your pessimism is a roadblock that will not let you move, consider reading Seligman's work or seeking extra help. Place "addressing your attitude" first on your professional goal list.

▶ *Exercise 3:*

Momentum

To "dislodge" my first portfolio display, I proposed to my partner we bring portfolio examples to our next presentation. I use each new interview or presentation as a chance to revamp and improve my portfolio. That momentum keeps me from going down the hill. There were certainly points at which I hit a plateau and needed another little push, but because I was caught up in the momentum, I was willing to push again. Use one, two, or all three of the following suggestions to keep your momentum going.

Planned Breather

How often do we give ourselves permission to relax? When you know you are going to have a rough, busy week or that you are just burnt out and need a vacation, a planned breather is the ticket. Do not plan any goals for one or two weeks. Place your standard goal sheet out of sight. Post instead the following three goals:

1. breathe
2. breathe
3. breathe again

By keeping the ritual of posting goals, you make it clear to your brain that you are not abandoning goal setting, projects, professional growth. This is just a breather; you are still on the quest. If you don't write these goals down, you are less likely to get back to writing goals later. If you write "breathe," you've given yourself permission to skip a week of working on the goal, but not to skip the ritual of writing three goals down.

Kick-in-the-Butt Starter

A kick-in-the-butt starter is exactly what it says it is. Find a way to put fire under your promise to reach a goal. Make a commitment to show something to your boss in a week. Bet your students you can finish your three goals or they get to pick out a special hat for you to wear next week. Tell a helpful busybody what you plan to accomplish, someone who will ask you in a crowded room, "Hey, Bill, how's your room remodeling going?" Nothing like a threatening kick in the butt to give you that initial burst of energy that gets the momentum flowing again.

Weeding Your List

When something on your three-step sheet remains on the sheet for longer than two weeks, question the item. Use your journal or support group to explore why you don't really want to do that particular activity. You may find out that it is not something you picked for yourself, that it is not actually a useful activity, or that it is just plain boring and you need to spruce it up. If you do not find an answer as to why that particular step is just hanging there, pick a new step from your map to work on. Professional development is so broad and interesting; there are always more avenues to pursue. Later that particular step might come easier.

▶ *Exercise 4:*
Proof of Accomplishments

Why is it so satisfying to clean your whole house at once, when it is not satisfying to clean parts of the house throughout the week or month? Isn't it because you can enjoy the finished product? The proof of all your hard work is right there in front of you. To keep yourself interested and motivated, gather proof of your accomplishments. I go into this step more in chapter 12, but right now you need to know that aiming for specific proof gives that extra oomph to your motivation.

> *To keep yourself interested and motivated, gather proof of your accomplishments.*

To generate a positive feeling about your professional growth plans, you must have some idea how you are going to prove that you accomplished the task. Of course, sometimes the task will offer its own proof. A report card from a finished class at the local university is proof. But what about when you plan to read a book or redesign your classroom?

Gold Star List of Accomplished Steps and Goals

The only long list you should have within your view is the Gold Star List of all that you have accomplished. That is a motivator! What is that list? you might ask. This list is not for the typical aspects of your work as a teacher. It is not the place to record "completed report cards" or "graded papers." These things you would do as a normal part of your routine as a teacher. The Gold Star List is for the things you did that pertain to your professional growth plans: "Started a journal"; "Organized a support group"; "Videotaped my lessons."

Display this list somewhere that you can see it every day; your display space would be perfect! Whenever you complete a goal or any objective, small or large, add it to the list and smile. Write the additions in bold letters on your list. Or draw pictures or use stamps to represent each goal. Or post your notes from a class, or put up before-and-after photographs. Like your journal, display space, and other elements of this process, personalize it. The list offers you a chance to acknowledge your growth, no matter how small it might be. You are on the move if you are adding to the list.

Proof of accomplishment will make your progress clear and exciting. Don't neglect the proof!

Part 3: Take Action

Finally

Before you leave this chapter I have to tell you one other thing. Surprise! You have already started! You have read this far in this book. The rock has been dislodged! If you have completed some or all of the exercises, the rock is rolling! If you have a journal or support group in place, half of your professional growth journey has been accomplished! If you have done the self-observation you are officially two-thirds the way down the hill!

Give yourself a pat on the back and recognize your accomplishments. You have taken great strides toward effecting your role as a teacher. Autonomy is an amazing self-motivator. The more you take charge over your development, the more motivated you will become to develop. The rest is just details!

Garden Lesson 1

He started working the soil one morning in May
(who knows what got into him).

Maybe it was the spicy food he'd eaten the night before
Maybe it was something in the air
Maybe it was just time
No matter.

He went to the corner drugstore for garden gloves
small tools and a large straw hat
to shade his eyes from
the blinding sun

and started digging. A snail-slow process, the ground
hard and idle so long. But he kept on.
These things take time.

Things take time.

—Kathleen Gumm

11
Staying on Track

The rung of ladder was never meant to rest upon, but only to hold a man's foot long enough to enable him to put the other somewhat higher.
—Thomas H. Huxley

Becoming a self-directed teacher means making a lifetime commitment to being your own person. In movies and stories, we see the theme repeatedly: Girl leaves home or leaves a person she loves. She travels the world trying different places, careers, or adventures, only to return home again where she is happy. Home is where she belongs.

Growing professionally is exactly like that. If it comes from within, if you make it part of you, then no matter how many times you neglect your goals or get off track or lose your balance, you will come back. You will come back because it is home. It is how you "see" yourself permanently. It is not a fleeting activity that you participate in for a little while then quit. No, it is the real you, and all the other distractions are just that—distractions.

I call this book a "guide" not a "plan." A diet "plan" means you gain a prepackaged list of foods you are to eat on any given day at any given meal, and when you go off the "plan," you have broken your diet and must start all over again. A food "guide" is a list of foods you need and that are good to eat. You decide when, where, and how you will proceed with your eating. You decide how much and how little of the guide you will incorporate into your life. You might even look for more information and ideas in other guides and materials. I encourage you to do so.

I want you to be a teacher who is autonomous and self-led. I believe many of the ideas and activities in this book complement one another and will assist a self-led individual. I also assume the more you learn and grow, the more you will leave behind the ideas of this book and create your own path. I also do not imagine any one teacher carrying out every specific idea from this book. That would be an enormous load to take on. If you put that kind of pressure on yourself, you are likely to lose interest out of exhaustion. Pick and choose and make your professional growth plan your own.

In light of how I see this book, a chapter called "staying on the right track" seems awkward and inappropriate. But it won't seem that way if you understand that the purpose of this chapter is to support your autonomy. "Staying on Track" simply means following your own plan.

Battling the Inner Saboteur

An inner saboteur is the little person inside some of us who is not interested in our growth and success. Often this little person is so deeply hidden, we do not know he is there until he destroys some perfectly good project that we were quite happy with. For instance, you get an invitation to come to an important community meeting to voice your opinion on youth issues. You are excited and flattered by this opportunity. Suddenly, the little saboteur creates lethargy in your limbs and you move so slowly that you are not only late for the meeting, your opportunity to speak has passed. Or perhaps you begin on a creative project in your spare time that you are enjoying immensely. But then you find yourself saying "yes" to all kinds of crazy commitments until all your free time is eaten away. Perhaps you do not have one of these saboteurs; congratulations. But if you recognize some inkling of yourself in what I say, then at least relax in knowing you are not alone.

I am not a psychologist with miles of information about your childhood influences and all the possible various reasons your saboteur exists. My sole purpose here is to give you some tools for dealing with the little guy. You don't need to give in to your "fear of failure" or your "impostor syndrome" thinking. Whatever is causing your self-sabotage, there are ways to get around the roadblocks. I'd like to give you a few exercises that have worked wonders on my various forms of self-sabotage.

▶ *Exercise 1:*
Stay on Target

If your saboteur is at work he will find ingenious ways to encourage you to change projects midstream, before you have achieved any measure of success. Plan to thwart his efforts by sticking with your plan until you reach a target discussed in the prior chapter before you consider changing directions. For instance, if you have decided to earn a master's degree and midway through your first semester, your saboteur begins to offer you other more promising ways to spend your time, ignore him. Write down those other ideas for future reference but do not stop what you are doing until you have reached your first target (which is probably completion of your first semester). When you have completed your target and have proof of success (a report card), then and only then may you consider changing directions or starting something new. This thwarts your saboteur, while still giving you room to be flexible in setting goals.

▶ *Exercise 2:*
Personify the Worry Monster

The little saboteur comes out in order to undermine your faith in your own capabilities. He whispers in your ear, "This is beyond you; you really shouldn't even bother to try." Whenever you hear the whispers, talk back: "You chicken!" Draw a picture of him and talk as if he were your boring, worrisome, tired, old Aunt Martha. "Yeah, whatever you say, Aunt Martha. You just sit here while I go out and make me a life." Amazing how personifying the worry monster can help you overcome your fears and limitations.

Part 3: Take Action

▶ *Exercise 3:*
Assume Positive Motives and Outcomes

When something negative happens or something positive does *not* happen, our little saboteurs take the opportunity to make us think the worst of the situation. For instance, you give a presentation and the audience is less than enthusiastic. You think, "They must not like me. I blew it. I have no business making this presentation anyway." To circumvent this saboteur, change your thinking. Explain the situation to your saboteur. "They were hot and tired, and I was the last to present." "They were actually overwhelmed and you left them with much to think about." And my personal favorite, "Let's ask what to change in order to improve it for the next time."

> *Dig deep to uncover the patterns and words that are undermining your success.*

Perhaps your saboteur is not so obvious. If you find you are repeatedly your own worse enemy, then dig deep to uncover the patterns and words that are undermining your success. That is your saboteur and you need to deal with him. If none of my approaches helps, make rules of your own.

Battling Others

As a teacher you will be getting input from many other people. It is as if everyone on this planet is your boss. Your students give you input, your principal and administrators give you input, mentor teachers give you input, even parents of students give you input. The general population hashes through what teachers should and should not do on a daily basis.

Everyone has spent some time in a classroom; everybody feels like a bit of a teaching expert. In some ways, everybody is a teaching expert. If each of us knows what worked and did not work in our own education then we each have some worthwhile ideas about teaching. Sure, some ideas may be biased, but not all ideas are without worth.

The problem is not that everyone has opinions and ideas. The problem is that others visit their opinions and ideas on teachers with the expectation that teachers will change. Your job, as an autonomous individual who makes choices and decisions regarding your classroom, is to measure the advice and requests against your own priorities.

What can you do when the requests are too numerous or do not fit with your plans as a teacher?

▶ *Exercise 4:*
Listen and Communicate

Perhaps the person making the request has a rationale that you can accommodate even if you cannot necessarily accommodate all of the idea. Perhaps the parent would be satisfied with a weekly phone report rather than a daily written report. Perhaps your principal would adjust a deadline so you can complete your theme unit first. Perhaps if you communicate what it is you are moving toward, critics will appreciate your efforts and expect less. In any case, there is no way to know without talk.

You might grimace and say, "Boy, you do not know my principal." If your principal is really so difficult, you might need to address that issue before anything else on your professional growth plan. Can you learn to communicate in a way that matches her style of thinking? Can you find other ways to influence her thinking? If she simply will never budge or offer you any sense of autonomy, perhaps it is time to look for another school. Autonomy is crucial to your fulfillment as a teacher.

▶ *Exercise 5:*
Evaluate the Source

Some people are overly critical because they have a hidden agenda that keeps them from helping you. Use your own instincts and perhaps the input of your support group to determine if you are dealing with such an individual. You do not want to give weight to criticism that is not stated to help you. Find a logical, nurturing person who will help you evaluate the situation. List five to ten criteria that will tell you if a person's criticism is meant to be constructive or merely a way to keep you from achieving a goal. Then write ten methods for cutting such discussions short: "Sorry, gotta go," whenever the topic turns to the criticized topic, for example.

▶ *Exercise 6:*
Learn to Say No

Sounds like a simplistic comeback, but you would be amazed how seldom people try it out. When someone makes a request that you believe is too much to accommodate your autonomy, ask for a day or so to think about the request. Then just say, "Nope. Sorry. Thanks for asking me, but I won't be able to do that." And let the other person come up with alternatives, unless you discover a way to meet the request; then make a revised proposal. More often than not, when you respond with a negative, supervisors and peers alike move on to find someone who hasn't learned to say no. It is not necessarily the fair method for dealing out work, but it is how it is done nevertheless.

▶ Exercise 7:
Share Your Goals

Often when you take the time to let those around know you have you own goals and objectives, they will look to support your efforts. People like to help other people. Give them a chance to help you.

Maintaining Your Balance

I am convinced that juggling is the gift of the twentieth century. When life meant your home and work were in the same place, juggling was not so much part of the equation. You didn't have to pick between family and job, work and home. They were one and the same, which probably made for a much slimmer margin of choice and freedom, but at least there was no juggling.

Now we have to make more choices. Sometimes it is a choice between important and more important. I remember the first time I had to call for a substitute in order to stay home with my sick child. Certainly my class needed me, but so did my child. It is not fun to have to pick between things you love. Nevertheless, it is the reality of current life, so we must deal with it.

It is the family that usually suffers in the juggling act because we can't get fired from home. Nevertheless, if we ignore our home life, work is bound to suffer at some point, too. Here are a few ideas for striking the balance.

1. **Marry Your Job:** If your job is your family, then you don't have to pick. Watching Mother Teresa on a documentary, I realized the incredible logic of the convent system. Nuns marry the church and do not have conventional families so they never have to balance their work with their family obligations. Of course, I would never expect other teachers to reject family life. I'm just saying it is one way to avoid having to balance the two!

2. **Treat Your Family as You Do Your Work:** Treat your family with the respect you provide your work. Give your family allotted time that is exclusively their time. You can do so in a number of ways.

    ▶ Make appointments every week and mark them on your calendar. My husband and I had a date every weekend until the baby-sitting expense grew too large. We are now working back into our regular dates and we have inspired many friends to do the same. It is a terrific marriage boost.

- ▶ Do all of your teaching work only at school. Being a teacher is like being a permanent student. Your work is never done, so if you bring it home you are likely to neglect your family for the work. Stay later at the school and finish it there, or leave what is unfinished.

3. **Ask Your Family to Chip In:** I know very few teachers whose children are not proficient paper graders and bulletin board makers! Include your family in your work and think of it as re-creating some small part of the intimacy of the nineteenth century.

Removing Roadblocks

How do you see challenges? Are they big, insurmountable walls standing in front of all of your dreams and aspirations? Are they too many or too few for your attention and focus? Do you have no goals, so you have no challenges? Or do you view challenges as exciting rites of passage as you move through life and growth?

Your perception of challenge is the key to removing roadblocks. Think of challenges as a game of chess; playing the game is the fun part. If you problem solve with relish, then all of your problems will become part of the joy of learning and growing. When problems seem insurmountable, do one or more of the following exercises:

▶ *Exercise 8:*
Brainstorm Solutions with a Friend (or Two or Three)

Help is a wonderful thing. You are suddenly no longer alone on your quest and the problem shrinks automatically.

▶ *Exercise 9:*
Try Something Different

Something about humans makes us do things over and over, even when they don't work. Deliberately make yourself think of something new to do, even if it seems silly.

▶ *Exercise 10:*
Skip a Challenge and Go to a Different One

The solution to the first challenge may come along when you are paying the least attention.

Maintaining Autonomy and Self-Directed Goal Setting

Self-motivated, self-planned improvement and success are a challenge. If they were not, there would not be such a market for self-help books and seminars. Many of us have the best intentions, but our efforts are often of the start-and-stop, start-and-stop variety. The biggest killer of progress is the statement: "Well, I blew it so now what is the use?" It is in this statement (or versions thereof) that we lose the war. So here are some personal improvement rules to follow.

1. I will start with whatever excites and motivates me; that is where I will create momentum. An object in motion remains in motion!
2. If I blow it, or backtrack, or have a bad week, I will not stay there. I will take a big breath, congratulate myself on the commitments I have made, the changes I have started upon, and my sheer resilience and willingness to get back on the road. I will reconfirm my commitment aloud to someone I trust and start again without regret.
3. I will confide in a listener, a cheerleader who can give me the emotional boost to keep going or to start again.
4. When I have even a small success, I shall share it with someone special.
5. I will celebrate as I cross my milestones on the road to success. I will keep a list of every success.

> *Motivation always comes back to one question: How well do you know yourself?*

Because autonomy comes from within, I cannot guarantee these rules will keep you on your own path. Motivation always comes back to one question: How well do you know yourself? The more self-aware and self-reflective you are, the better chances you have of motivating yourself. The only method I recommend is to keep trying; do not drop the ball.

Staying in Place

Some white flowers
without a name grew along a bank
I saw them as I was traveling home

and the going was slow

Cars and trucks
hurried past the sun lying low
the fruit stands full of oranges
peaches and greens on a two lane
highway narrow and long
with a sign that read
Use Headlights During Daylight Hours

The wind
scented with farm grass
and night closing in
was a summer wind, unsettling
my convictions, still I was heading
back to my place called home

and the going was slow.

—Kathleen Gumm

12

Assess Yourself

I don't know the key to success, but the key to failure is to try to please everyone.

—Bill Cosby

Assess Yourself

You have examined your aspirations and challenges as a teacher; you have listed changes you want to make; you have even started on at least one small project. As a professional teacher, you know an important key to your growth is the feedback you receive from yourself and others. If there is no point at which you receive notice about how you are improving or declining, then you are unlikely to do much growing. Feedback is essential to the learning process.

When I started teaching, I had a very nice principal who was just three years shy of retirement. The school was large and he had a tremendous amount of work and daily interactions. He came into my class a few times at the very beginning of the school year and made slight comments about changing a bulletin board here or seating the children differently there. The sum of his feedback on my teaching was a few nondescript sentences at the end of the school year. He didn't neglect me in order to be mean. He assured me he was confident in my abilities, so he spent his time in more urgent situations. To some degree he felt his lack of attention was a compliment. For me, this lack of feedback was a big, black hole. How could I improve as a teacher without evaluation, without assessment?

> **Feedback is essential to the learning process.**

This experience was frustrating to me, but later I realized the problem was not that my principal did not give me clear feedback. The problem was that I was waiting for some system of feedback to just happen, without any input from me. What kind of feedback did I want? When did I want the feedback to happen? How would I like to be assessed on my progress?

What about this method of assessing your success as a teacher? Your students are in charge of deciding whether you are doing a good job or not. They experience your lesson, finish their independent or group work, then let you know about your performance by giving you a report card. Such an assessment would offer a different perspective than would a principal evaluation. But would it, on its own, be a reliable method of feedback? While some students may have an extremely good handle on areas in which you are strong and areas you need to improve, some will not. Many students will judge you based on their mood of the day, if they like your outfit, on whether you made the test easy or not. They won't necessarily relate their successful learning to your awesome teaching. While you are teaching a particularly difficult session of learning material, many students might find you too difficult and pushy. Meanwhile they would give you outstanding grades on recess and physical education.

What about using a multiple-choice exam to evaluate your teaching skill and knowledge? How many of us would be willing to be evaluated solely on an exam where we choose A, B, C, or D, none of the above?

Part 3: Take Action

> *Your students are pounding their desks with their fists, demanding to leave school and go home early. None of your calls for discipline are working. Do you*
>
> A. *Cry*
> B. *Call the principal to take over; you are going home for the day.*
> C. *Open the door and smile broadly at each student as they leave.*
> D. *None of the above.*

I once passed a multiple choice exam that firefighters take as part of a government employment program. I was relieved to learn firefighters also have to take more practical tests. It is comical to imagine me driving a fire truck based solely on a multiple choice exam!

But where does rejecting these methods leave assessment? How can we best get the feedback we need as teachers to do our jobs properly and to progress and improve at teaching over the course of our careers? We need assessment options that give us multiple perspectives, general and specific feedback, and a reliable means for determining what future projects we should take on. All of the assessment formulas that I discuss above may be useful for different parts of your personal assessment method. The key is using a great variety of feedback and assessment mechanisms with a central processing agent: you.

Certainly, if I have spent the first twelve chapters of this book advocating that teachers take over their professional planning, it is not surprising that I also advocate self-directed forms of assessment. I don't mean that you should never seek help from anyone else; quite to the contrary. Nor do I think you should replace your district- and school-based evaluations. Principal, student, peer, and other points of view are valuable and should nicely complement the methods you design to evaluate yourself.

What I advocate is that, in addition to any teacher assessment mechanisms already in place at your school, you create your own. You determine what will be evaluated and how it will be evaluated. Do not drop the ball on autonomy at this point in your professional development. Do not be at the mercy of the possibly fickle interests or priorities of others. Instead, decide what is most important about your development as a teacher, then decide how to measure and assess your progress in that area.

This chapter gives you a number of possible methods for assessing your progress. For your convenience and to meet all your needs, some of the methods are quick and easy; some are medium-range assessments; some are long term and complex. I encourage you to develop a wide variety methods to get the best possible feedback.

▶ *Exercise 1:*
The Box

The easiest, fastest way to get started on your assessment journey is to begin collecting evidence of your teaching growth and success. Early in my teaching life, a mentor took me aside and said, "Get a box and collect important stuff in it. Any brochures you have from speaking engagements, example lesson plans, copies of student projects you designed, notes from students and parents. Save all of that stuff in a big old box. You will be glad you have it later, trust me."

I found "the box" easy to do. I could even use a Tupperware box so it wouldn't look too unappealing. The box actually helped me because I really hated to toss wonderful notes from students or certificates from courses I had completed, but I never knew where to file all that stuff. Now I had a box.

Get your box now and begin to save. Later, when you have the time, energy, or motivation to display, evaluate, and organize you items, everything you need will be right there, in your box. Plus it is so much fun to go through your old stuff. It brings up wonderful memories and makes you wonder about all the students who have crossed your path—definitely a soul-building activity. The first time you finally pull out and begin to go through your box, you will begin to see the holes in your collection. "Gosh, I have no good examples of students projects." Or "I never actually ask for feedback from my students or their parents." These holes can be the beginnings of more specific assessment designs.

▶ *Exercise 2:*
Indicators and Criteria

Indicators are the materials and proof you intend to gather as evidence of your growth or improvement. I discussed them in chapter 11. Indicators for project-oriented goals are fairly easy to identify. If you plan to create a teacher web site to increase parent-teacher communication, then the finished site itself would be the indicator. Create a file copy of the homepage of your web site and your Internet address. Then evaluate your work based on criteria you design. If, however, you target a process-oriented goal, then you must get a little more creative when designing your indicator. If you say you want to establish better rapport with other teachers, you might not have an exact piece of evidence that will show that you have improved your social and professional interactions. However, you could demonstrate your commitment to this goal by saving the agenda from your first teacher support group meeting or taking a photo of your support group. Or you might ask your principal or an unbiased party to evaluate how well you have met this goal. The key is deciding in advance what will be the proof of your progress, then retaining the proof for your own records.

Part 3: Take Action

> **Create a list of things you are going to use for evaluating your work.**

Deciding what indicators will help you truly assess your growth is only the first step in the evaluation process. You also need to know how you are going to "grade." If, for instance, you are designing a theme unit as a project-oriented goal, then how are you going to decide if it is a good theme unit? Certainly, creating a copy of the unit as an indicator of your work is a good starting place. But you must have some criteria for judging the finished product. Side-by-side with selecting indicators is making decisions about how to evaluate your own work. Will you measure it against the work of someone else? Will you ask a friend or peer or mentor to evaluate the work for you? These are potential options.

I recommend an additional possible method. Create a list of things, a kind of rubric, you are going to use for evaluating your work. For instance, to evaluate a web page, you might say it must have the following:

at least five subtopics for visitors to explore

an area specifically of interest to parents

a well-thought-out and easy-to-use format

a place where parents and students can comment or ask you to contact them

evidence that you let parents know the site was available to them

Understand you are using these criteria to grade your own ability to design and successfully implement your teacher web page. Your criteria will give you the framework you need to address as you proceed. You would keep the indicator (web page printout) and your own evaluation of your work as a record of your success. You would also add any notes or comments you receive from parents or students and the method you used to publicize the page.

Or say your goal is to increase student motivation; you decide to gather two different indicators: a before-and-after survey and documentation of decreased discipline problems. Your criteria are relatively spelled out within the indicators. In the "after" survey, do a larger number of students say they were motivated and interested in the activity? Did classroom discipline problems decrease?

Figures 3 and 4 show examples of project- and process-goal evaluation charts. Such charts give you a clear picture of what you are aiming to achieve before you embark on your plan. Use similar charts for any goal before you take action. You will find that this type of preparation pays large dividends because you have thoroughly thought out what you wish to achieve. It works the same way as telling your students what is ahead on the "test" or project. You suddenly become attuned to the key points that you must keep in mind. The charts themselves can also be included as part of your records.

Assess Yourself

Evidence of Progress

Goals	Objectives/Steps	Potential Indicators	Criteria
Example: 1. Develop parent communication tools	1. Publish a class newsletter. 2. Parent phone calls.	1. Copy of newsletter/comments from parents. 2. Phone log.	1. Put out 4 per year. Did it communicate class activities? Did parents think it was useful? 2. Even ratio of positive to negative calls?
2.			
3.			

Figure 3. Project-goal evaluation chart

Evidence of Progress

Goals	Actions	Potential Indicators	Criteria
Example: 1. Reduce student stress and threat in the classroom.	1. Get ideas from friends. 2. Ask Jill Smith if I can observe her style. 3. Add humor and music to class.	1. Notes from brainstorm with friends 2. Observation notes on reducing stress 3. Joke sessions in AM; Mozart	1. Did I use ideas in class? Evaluate if helped 2. Same as 1 3. How did students respond to jokes and music?
2.			
3.			

Figure 4. Process-goal evaluation chart

You do not have to carefully establish indicators and criteria for every single goal. However, I recommend designing and writing out indicators and criteria for at least a few large-scale goals. With a little practice, designing indicators and criteria will become second nature.

One special note of caution: The indicators and criteria you select ought to feel like authentic ways to judge your own progress. Don't destroy your intrinsic motivation by choosing insincere methods of evaluating yourself. For instance, you have a goal to start a teacher support group. You never start the group, but you hold on to friendly notes from other teachers as if you had met your goal. Better to choose no methods than to choose something that is not truly relevant to your goals.

Part 3: Take Action

▶ Exercise 3:
The Short Survey

Short surveys are designed primarily as a device for checking student opinion and feelings. If you are targeting some specific classroom changes, often a quick before-and-after survey will give you an idea of how students received those changes. You can do quick surveys on paper or orally. They are particularly effective if your goal is process oriented, such as increasing student motivation, developing improved questioning techniques, or decreasing stress and threat in the classroom. Develop short surveys for a variety of your goals.

▶ Exercise 4:
Video

The video is useful not only for observation, but also for evaluation and assessment. It is such a useful tool because it does not require anything more than the camera and a table or tripod to get the correct angle. Reviewing videos has real value to the teacher and keeping those that show progress over time is an upbeat, exciting assessment tool. Set up a camcorder on a tripod in your class, or ask a colleague or parent to videotape you.

▶ Exercise 5:
Self-Analysis

Set up a regular time to look through your journals and classroom documentation. It might be once a week, once a month, once a year, or every reporting period. Jot down notes about where you have improved and areas that you need to address. Sometimes something as simple as expressing your thoughts on paper has a domino effect. You may find that over time, certain complaints disappear from your journal, which is generally a sign that you have overcome the problem.

▶ Exercise 6:
Your Gold Star List of Achievements

In time you will want to have more complete indicators and criteria as part of your evidence of growth. But for smaller goals and to get started, the Gold Star List discussed in the previous chapter will do nicely. At least you can say you have done everything on that list. The list itself identifies your progress.

▶ *Exercise 7:*
Parent and Student Evaluations

Look for parent and student feedback as one more tool in your professional assessment bag. The book *How Am I Teaching* (Weimer, Parrett, and Kerns 1988) has many ideas for surveys and evaluations you can pass out to students and parents. Use these surveys as examples for your own. If you teach elementary or middle school, simplify the vocabulary but maintain the content.

Parents and students are often pleasantly surprised the teacher has any interest in their opinions. They are more than happy to share their thoughts on you as a teacher. But be careful not to get hung up on the one parent or student who may have issues you cannot resolve. Look more for patterns of opinions, and of course, always believe the compliments!

Many teachers also ask the students or parents to give them report cards on their teaching. If you design a teacher report card, don't forget to ask students to fill it out at least twice during the year so you can work on improving throughout the year. If you do it only at the end of the year, students will not experience the benefits of your improvement. Develop an appropriate tool for you to use.

▶ *Exercise 8:*
Observation Feedback

At most school sites administrators do observe, but sometimes they decrease or eliminate their observation of experienced teachers. If you are experienced but think your principal has good feedback to offer, ask her to resume or continue observation as a professional courtesy. You can even design very specific feedback forms to get the specific information you want. If you continue to get regular principal evaluations, add these to your assessment kit. They are one more way to examine and plan for professional goals.

▶ *Exercise 9:*
The Portfolio

The portfolio arises from a proactive way of thinking that leads to a conscious collection of logical examples and materials. Portfolios are a well-respected form of tracking and assessing professional progress in many professions. Essentially, a portfolio is an organized presentation of the various assessment options discussed in this chapter.

The first step in organizing a portfolio is choosing general categories for which you want to collect evidence. You might use the domains identified on page 57 or your school district's framework for professional development. Or you might develop your own categories. As you collect indicators, surveys, videotapes, and so on, organize items into your portfolio categories. When a category appears, you may want to design some assessment options and include them in your portfolio, or you may choose not to focus on assessment right then. Your final portfolio might be in a binder, notebook, or giant artist's portfolio. It might include samples of everything mentioned in this chapter as well as lesson plans, student work samples, and notes and cards from students, parents, and colleagues. Consider it your album of professional growth. Weed out items and change your portfolio as you grow and change. Or at some point, close it. Put it in your teacher library and start the process again. These bits and pieces of evidence are indicators.

Summer Vacation

*Our hellos
finally stand true now
that summer has come
now that good-byes intrude
on the ground from which came
such paper fruit
And became a shaded orchard
It may have been the laughter, or
the secrets we could not keep
It could have been that you saw
your life in my print and I saw
mine in yours, the occasional
verbs, the proper nouns swelling
echoing, filling in the gaps.*

*Now stretches long and green
the land between us, the months, the miles
Until September is come.*

—Kathleen Gumm

13
Celebrate

In everyone's life, at some time, our inner fire goes out. It is then burst into flame by an encounter with another human being. We should all be thankful for those people who rekindle the inner spirit.

—Albert Schweitzer

Part 3: Take Action

Teacher Appreciation Week is a big event in my school district. It comes at the end of every year just before (or right after) open house. Parents want to acknowledge all of the hard work teachers put in throughout the year, so they arrange a week-long celebration. They plan special teacher surprises for every day of the week. Mondays students bring fresh flowers from home in a special vase. Tuesdays might be the day students bring in special notes to their teachers. Wednesdays, special treats appear in the staff room. And so on throughout the week. Generally, it all ends with some special kind of culminating activity. Sometimes it all seems like a bit much. Each year outshine the previous year. But one thing can certainly be said: teachers feel noticed and appreciated!

> **We need to acknowledge our growth even as we make plans to move further ahead.**

Humans love rites of passage. We mark our growth and progress with such rites. We celebrate birthdays and anniversaries, New Year's and the start of spring. We like to mark changes. I believe we also *need* to mark changes.

This brief chapter is dedicated to encouraging you to mark your changes and giving you some thoughts and ideas of ways to celebrate. Part of progressing means looking back and acknowledging what you have accomplished. Isn't that why graduation ceremonies are often filled with reminiscing as much as looking forward? We need to acknowledge our growth even as we make plans to move further ahead.

When my own children finish a particularly grueling bit of homework we "high five." When they learn a new piano piece we gather around to listen. When they learn a number of pieces, their piano teacher holds a recital. All of these count as celebrations in my book. As you plan your professional growth goals, don't forget to include all kinds of milestone markers and celebrations.

Brainstorm with your support group or partner, write in your journal, or just start a running list of ideas for ways to acknowledge and celebrate your successes. Be sure to prepare ideas for all kinds of celebrations, everything from short, sweet acknowledgments to big call-all-your-friends-and-party celebrations. Such celebrations are not rewards, but more like place markers—"I am now right here on my journey." Think of each of these moments or events as a chance to

1. Acknowledge your progress
2. Thank anyone who has helped you on the way
3. Share with others what you are trying to do
4. Build energy and momentum for your next step

Quickie Celebrations

Short, sweet celebrations help mark an event and give you a spurt of energy for the next hurdle. They are the easiest to take on, but also the easiest to neglect. Somehow we fall into the pattern of preparing only for the "big" moments, the graduations and certifications, rather than the "job-well-dones" and "I am prouds." Following are some of my ideas for quickie acknowledgments:

▶ *Exercise 1:*
The Gold Star List

The very first and foremost quickie form of celebration is to put your accomplishment on your Gold Star List. You may have already developed a list as part of your proof of accomplishments earlier. If not, consider adding it now as an easy way to celebrate completing your steps.

▶ *Exercise 2:*
A Support Group or Classroom Cheer

Incorporate a cheer into your classroom routine. It doesn't have to be silly or crazy a round of applause works fine. Allow individual students to have a moment to voice some recent success or progress they have made, then as a class, give them a cheer that you have developed together. Be sure you use this ritual as a place to announce your progress as a teacher and allow your students to send you a warm cheer to acknowledge your progress. Don't forget to thank your students, if doing so is in order.

You can also incorporate the cheer into your support group routine. At the end of meetings, allow for quick acknowledgments and follow with a group cheer. Doing so allows everyone in the group to feel good about the success of others and identifies points of progress.

▶ *Exercise 3:*
Five Minutes of Congratulations

Five Minutes is similar to a cheer except it is delivered more personally. For instance, small student groups can take five minutes to notice and congratulate others in the group on recent accomplishments. Your teacher support group can do the same. Another way to deliver the Five Minutes of Congratulations is to have a cocktail party where everyone in the group or room wanders around talking to others for five or fewer minutes. All individuals should drop by at least three different people, share successes and progress, and congratulate each other with words, a handshake, or a high five.

Part 3: Take Action

▶ *Exercise 4:*
The Unplanned Share

Sometimes we cannot think of any short rituals that we are comfortable instituting. The unplanned share is a perfect alternative if you do not want a regular cheer or congratulations cocktail party. The unplanned share is random. When you complete some professional growth project or goal, or when you feel you have improved in some aspect of teaching that you deem important, even if it is only a short success, share it. Share it with someone who will smile and pat you on the back. Use your spouse, family members, friends, other teachers, your principal, or, yes, even your students. Call home to mom or make a quick visit to your best friend's house.

Some people will say, "Oh, no, that is bragging. I couldn't do that." We have been raised to believe it is wrong to boast or brag. However, I believe a short expression of personal pride is a roadway to intimacy. People who are close to you want to know about your personal successes. By sharing with them, you let them into your inner thoughts and personal triumphs. Bragging is different: individuals go on and on about themselves or their families to get an inordinate amount of attention. Or they try to prove they are superior to everyone else. Asking a close friend or even your students to acknowledge your growth with you is merely sharing your progress. If you find your "sharing" causes discomfort to someone, find another someone to share with. But don't condemn all successful endeavors to the closet.

Bigger Celebrations

Bigger celebrations take a little more planning an preparation but are well worth your attention. By planning for a bigger celebration, you pay increased notice to your accomplishments, which gives you (1) a larger sense of self-satisfaction and (2) a chance to communicate your progress to an audience.

▶ *Exercise 5:*
Piggyback Celebrations

Use an occasion or ceremony set aside to celebrate something else to acknowledge some of your successes. For instance the first day of school celebration, back-to-school nights, and open houses are terrific opportunities for teachers to let parents and students know some of the things they have been working on to improve their teaching. You might make an announcement or create a display about a recently finished project, then announce the next challenge you plan to take on. By seeing your goals and successes, your students and parents will have a better handle on who you are as a teacher; they may even be motivated to help out. In addition, such self-affirmation is tremendous modeling for your students. They need to know that even in adulthood there will be more challenges and learning.

> *People who are close to you want to know about your personal successes.*

▶ *Exercise 6:*
Displays

I encourage you to have, in addition to your personal display space, a display space for acknowledging success. You can post your gold star list, as I said before, but you can also post other evidence of your progress. Let's say one of your goals is to make your room environment more conducive to learning. Perhaps you add plants, rearrange furniture for better traffic flow, and add a quiet reading area. You could post pictures of your changes in your display area with a caption that reads, "Now isn't that a little nicer?" Let your students post their responses to your posting.

Bigger displays might be appropriate for ongoing projects or processes. If one of your goals is to increase the variety of art lessons, you could create a gallery of the year's various art assignments. You and your students will enjoy the overview of what has been accomplished. You may want to create a display of your professional growth goals and accomplishments to share your growth with parents and students. Set the display up at the beginning of the school year as a preview of what is to come, at the end of the school year, or even as part of parent conferences.

A web page is also a great place to display your progress on your professional growth goals. When parents and students tune in, they find out you are proud of your own growth as well as the growth of your students.

▶ *Exercise 7:*
Presentations

If the accomplishment of your goal leads to something worth sharing with other teachers, then perhaps a presentation is in order. You can share and celebrate your newly acquired knowledge or skills by becoming a workshop presenter. We learn best by teaching something ourselves, so present to others and to retain what you learned! In the process you will be celebrating by sharing.

Summer

Summer...
She drew me in
to her golden cave
painted my sky with fiction.

Through the days
I lingered long upon
the lakes edge, listening
to the voice of blue-water and content

but someone found out
where we were hiding—

Now Autumn
He's after us both.

—Kathleen Gumm

14

Pass the Word

Here is the test to find whether your mission on earth is finished. If you're alive, it isn't.

—Richard Bach

You are a teacher. You picked up and read this book because you believe in aspiring to greater heights. The ultimate measure of what you can accomplish as a teacher is your teaching. Are you able to pass your messages along to your students, within your school, within the world of education, and perhaps even in the political arena?

Teachers and schools are often affected by politics. There are politics within the school and there are politics around the school. If we care about our students and we care about education, we must not ignore the world of politics; we must take it on.

You might be saying, "Wait one minute; I am no leader. I'm shy. I became a teacher because I love kindergarten children, not noisy, boisterous political parties." Leadership comes in many packages. This chapter is about encouraging you to answer the call for leadership without losing the essence of who you are. We are all able to lead in our own ways; we simply must discover those ways and choose to lead.

One school year I had the privilege of teaching Jorge. He was an interesting student. He was a large child, taller and wider than any of his classmates, but the same age as the rest of the fifth graders. In many schools and classes, cruel children would have dubbed Jorge "Porky" or some other insulting nickname. Not in my class or school. The students liked and respected him.

Jorge had a special kind of leadership ability that taught me much about what causes people to follow. He was about average in school achievement. He was very soft spoken and seldom offered his opinion unless called upon. He was not part of the popular crowd or particularly athletic. But after about the second week of school, I noticed the strangest transition in my classroom.

Students would be in a heated debate with no hope of agreeing; they would turn to Jorge. He had this terrific way of listening to both sides of the discussion while just sitting quietly, then would continue to sit after everyone else was through talking. He paused for so long, but students waited, then were enamored by his every word when he did speak. Often, he just repeated what had already been said, but because he removed judgment or tone or attitude, the two sides were finally able to reach a consensus. He did this so naturally and so often that, frankly, it took me months to realize what a splendid leader he was. I found myself automatically placing him with struggling or difficult students, and the groups inevitably improved. Jorge was a tremendous help in the classroom.

Leaders come in all kinds of packages. Can you really compare the leadership style of Mother Teresa to that of Winston Churchill? Or of Robert Kennedy to that of Joan of Arc? Many leaders are not people we initially think of as leaders, like Jorge, but they prove to influence others through their behavior, attitude, ability to listen, or empathize.

I don't suggest you try to lead in all situations. There may be a time when you are more effective as a follower than as a leader. But there will be times when you will want to take up the banner, and it will help you know what your leading strengths are. Finding those strengths is what this chapter is all about.

▶ *Exercise 1:*
Identifying Leaders

Leaders are people who have independent thoughts and feel empowered to communicate and act upon their opinions. Leaders may be found in the classroom, as part of a committee, in an elected or assigned position of authority, or even in an independent working situation. Leaders have vision and purpose and action. They are courageous about stepping up to the plate and influencing the future. What makes them leaders is not their roles, but their choices to act.

List people in your family, school, and community who you think have a vision and make a real impact. You may know someone who leads from a quiet place, influencing decisions by living according to his vision and communicating it to others. You may also know leaders who are opinionated and forthright, who act on decisions. You may know leaders who hold positions of authority. Separate the idea of leadership from that of authority. Leaders are more like coaches. They communicate a vision clearly. They inspire others to join forces and make a vision happen. Leaders are open to changing the vision if the situation requires it. And real leaders behave ethically even when it is unpopular or personally difficult.

> *Leaders have vision and purpose and action.*

Once you have thought of everyone you can, choose ten names from your list. Look closely at those ten names and ask yourself what they have in common. You may come up with a list that has many of the following qualities:

- They act; they do not wait to be acted upon.
- They feel empowered and capable. They do not complain.
- They communicate their idea of what is important, of their purpose.
- They live by their convictions.

These qualities will lead you to form an opinion of what the general concept of leadership means to you. Then think about how the people on your list do it. What actions do they take to lead? Leadership style is very personal, and there are many types of leaders. Following are descriptions of a few leadership styles that may help you evaluate the styles of the people on your list.

Clandestine Leader

My brother-in-law is a clandestine leader. He is a cartoonist by nature, banker by profession. Throughout his life and a multitude of careers, he has used his special sense of humor and drawing abilities to entertain and call attention to details at the places where he works. He draws cartoons and posts them on the work bulletin space. He communicates his opinion about idiosyncrasies of the workplace while delivering a smile. Other clandestine leaders use letters or notes, or they write books or create works of art. The power of their leadership is defined within the power of their expression. They choose to influence the process and encourage a vision for change by using a vehicle other than an overt leadership role.

The Outspoken Leader

This individual uses the podium to communicate a vision. She is someone whom you will find accepting committee chairships and developing alliances. She is never, however, too opinionated to avoid listening.

Group Leaders

This leader joins a ready-made organization or gathers together people who share interests. Together they develop an action plan to make the vision real.

I'm sure you can think of many more types of leaders. Your list may give rise to many of them.

▶ *Exercise 2:*
Finding Your Leadership Style

Do you remember a time you led? You stood behind a vision or an ideal, and you inspired others to join you. How did it feel? It might have been frightening. It takes courage to support and pursue what you believe. Remember that each time you lead, you gain confidence and courage for the next time.

Define the ways you communicated your ideas and vision. How did others receive it? Perhaps you see yourself as having more than one style. Perhaps you take different approaches in different circumstances. Know which approach will work for you and give it a try. Try more than one.

Begin formulating a vision. Imagine various ways to communicate that vision to others. Are you likely to lead a team effort? Are you happier behind the scenes, stirring up interest? Whatever your choices, begin. Communicate and express your ideals and remember to listen. Your vision may be honed by the wise input of other leaders on your path. You may need to identify fears that hold you back. But don't let them limit the scope of your action. Remember that every leader in history has made mistakes and had failures. Lincoln ran for office a number of times before he actually won an election. Choosing not to try does damage to your soul.

▶ *Exercise 3:*
Kick Start Your Vision

Imagine three headlines about education, your school, or your classroom that you would like to see in print. If you opened your morning paper and read one of these headlines, would you be ecstatic? Begin your leadership journey with those headlines; they are possible visions.

Claire

*The years between us
were an offering
laid down
next to the bread
the burgundy-velvet wine*

*I tasted her life
her struggles, the early years
through her words
imagining the rough canvasses
she had painted on—*

*wings of an artist
taking flight above
the speckled fields of duty*

*while I, yet as a bird's
shadow on the grass, having
glimpsed her September sky, knew*

One day I too would fly.

—Kathleen Gumm

Resources

Teacher Tools

Cameron, Julia. *The Artist's Way.*
> Cameron leads participants on a self-discovery journey that lasts twelve weeks. I recommend working with a partner on one chapter per week.

Klauser, Henriette Anne. *Writing on Both Sides of the Brain.*
> If you have never fully realized the benefits of journal writing, Klauser's activities will help you discover your muse and never experience writer's block again.

Caine, Geoffrey, Renate Numella Caine, and Sam Crowell. *MindShifts.*
> The Caines have created a book that you can use in groups to process and share your educational experiences.

Classroom Connect: http://www.classroom.net/
> This Internet site offers teacher chat groups and support networks as well as quick answers to any teacher questions that haunt you.

Self-Discovery and Personal Reflection (Heart and Soul)

Sher, Barbara. *Wishcraft.*
> This book is for people who wonder if they are on the right life path. The activities are easy, fun, and extremely enlightening.

Moore, Thomas. *Care of the Soul.*
> Moore's book is philosophical and thoughtful. It aims to help readers understand the nature of soul and offers ways to nurture the deep self.

Eyre, Linda, and Richard Eyre. *Lifebalance.*
> The Eyres provide wonderful activities and a framework for getting to the heart of what is most important on your to do list. Short and easy to read.

Self-Directed Learning and Planning

Covey, Stephen. *The Seven Habits of Highly Effective People.*
> Covey's book has been on the best-seller list for more than a decade. It takes readers on a self-exploration and offers a series of planning tools that force personal examination of priorities and lifestyle. I find the planning tools a little overwhelming, but the messages are profound.

Gross, Ronald. *Peak Learning.*
> Gross, an avid proponent of self-directed schooling, helps you plan out your educational path.

Csikszentmihalyi, Mihaly. *Flow.*
> Csikszentmihalyi shares his extensive research into the nature of happiness. A core message is that developing autonomy and choosing our own goals are keys to fulfilling lives.

Danielson, Charlotte. *Enhancing Professional Practice.*
> Danielson's book provides a clear framework for improving in all areas of your teaching.

Evaluation and Assessment

Weimer, Maryellen, Joan L. Parrett, and Mary-Margaret Kerns. *How Am I Teaching?*
> This book is filled with surveys to give to students to evaluate your teachings. Many words and designs may have to be simplified for younger students, but the book is filled with ideas you can easily adjust to fit your own priorities.

Danielson, Charlotte. *Enhancing Professional Practice.*
> Danielson's book provides a framework and gives specific rubric for assessing your improvement and performance in each area of teaching.

Leadership

Bennis, William, and Joan Goldsmith. *Learning to Lead.*
> Bennis and Goldsmith use this workbook format to help readers examine their concept of leadership. The authors give ways to develop and hone leadership skills.

Bibliography

Armstrong, Thomas. 1998. *Awakening Genius in the Classroom.* Alexandria, Va.: Association for Supervision and Curriculum Development.

Bennis, Warren, and Joan Goldsmith. 1994. *Learning to Lead: A Workbook on Becoming a Leader.* Reding, Mass.: Addison-Wesley.

Caine, Renate Nummela, and Geoffrey Caine. 1997. *Education on the Edge of Possibility.* Alexandria, Va.: Association for Supervision and Curriculum Development.

Caine, Geoffrey, Renate Nummela Caine, and Sam Crowell. 1994. *MindShifts: A Brain-Based Process for Restructuring Schools and Renewing Education.* Tucson, Ariz.: Zephyr Press.

Cameron, Julia. 1992. *The Artist's Way: A Spiritual Path to Higher Creativity.* New York: G. P. Putnam's.

Covey, Stephen R. 1989. *The Seven Habits of Highly Effective People.* New York: Simon and Schuster.

Csikszentmihalyi, Mihalyi. 1990. *Flow: The Psychology of Optimal Experience.* New York: Harper and Row.

Danielson, Charlotte. 1996. *Enhancing Professional Practice: A Framework for Teaching.* Alexandria, Va.: Association for Supervision and Curriculum Development.

Deci, Edward L. 1995. *Why We Do What We Do.* New York: G. P. Putnam's.

DesRoches, Brian. 1995. *Your Boss Is Not Your Mother: Creating Autonomy, Respect, and Success at Work.* New York: William Morrow.

Eyre, Linda, and Richard Eyre. 1997. *Lifebalance: How to Simplify and Bring Harmony to Your Everyday Life.* New York: Fireside.

Fried, Robert L. 1995. *The Passionate Teacher: A Practical Guide.* Boston: Beacon Press.

Gardner, Howard. 1991. *The Unschooled Mind: How Children Think and How Schools Should Teach.* New York: Basic.

Glasser, William. 1993. *The Quality School Teacher: A Companion Volume to* The Quality School. New York: HarperPerennial.

Goleman, Daniel. 1995. *Emotional Intelligence: Why It Can Matter More than IQ.* New York: Bantam.

Gross, Ronald. 1991. *Peak Learning: How to Create Your Own Lifelong Education Program for Personal Enjoyment and Professional Success.* New York: G. P. Putnam's.

Hargreaves, Andy, ed. 1997. *Rethinking Educational Change with the Heart and Mind: 1997 ASCD Yearbook*. Alexandria, Va.: Association for Supervision and Curriculum Development.
Hemphill, Barbara. 1997. *Taming the Paper Tiger.* Washington, D.C.: Kiplinger Washington Editors.
Highet, Gilbert. 1989. *The Art of Teaching.* New York: Vintage.
Jensen, Eric. 1994. *The Learning Brain.* San Diego: Turning Point Publishing.
———. 1998. *Teaching with the Brain in Mind.* Alexandria, Va.: Association for Supervision and Curriculum Development.
John-Steiner, Vera. 1997. *Notebooks of the Mind: Explorations of Thinking.* New York: Oxford University Press.
Klauser, Henriette Anne. 1987. *Writing on Both Sides of the Brain: Breakthrough Techniques for People Who Write.* New York: HarperCollins.
———. 1995. *Putting Your Heart on Paper: Staying Connected in a Loose-Ends World.* New York: Bantam.
Miller, Alice. 1981. *The Drama of the Gifted Child: The Search for the True Self.* New York: Basic.
Moore, Thomas. 1992. *Care of the Soul: A Guide for Cultivating Depth and Sacredness in Everyday Life.* New York: HarperCollins.
Moreau, Daniel. 1996. *Take Charge of Your Career.* Washington, D.C.: Kiplinger Times.
Seligman, Martin E. P. 1996. *The Optimistic Child: A Proven Program to Safeguard Children against Depression and Build Lifelong Resilience.* New York: HarperPerennial.
Sher, Barbara. 1979. *Wishcraft: How to Get What You Really Want.* New York: Ballantine.
Weimer, Maryellen, Joan L. Parrett, and Mary-Margaret Kerns. 1988. *How Am I Teaching? Forms and Activities for Acquiring Instructional Input.* Madison, Wis.: Magna.

Internet Sites

Classroom Connect (offers chat groups, support networks, quick answers to any teacher question that haunts you): http://www.classroom.net/
National Education Association (includes many useful links): http://www.nea.org/
Association of Supervision and Curriculum Development (includes useful links, training, and ongoing educational discussions): http://www.ascd.org/
National Education Service (includes many useful links and a teacher chat bulletin board): http://www.nes.org/
Gateway (offers lessons organized by grade and subject area): http://www.thegateway.org/
Education World (easy to use, lesson and study links, teacher bulletin board): http://www.education-world.com
The Busy Teacher's Website (filled with links to useful educational sites): http://www.ceismc.gateech.edu/busyt/

Get started in MI—it's easy with this handy resource from the author of Three Cheers for Teaching!

MULTIPLE INTELLIGENCES MADE EASY
Strategies for Your Curriculum
by Bonita DeAmicis
Grades 3–6

Get started in MI right now with 43 easy-to-use lessons and strategies. You'll be linking each intelligence to your curriculum in convenient daily doses—even if you have no experience with MI. Look to this valuable resource for effective MI strategies to fill out your daily lessons, including—

- Visual-spatial—visualization, redrawing from memory
- Musical-rhythmic—choral writing, background music, math music
- Bodily-kinesthetic—role plays, body as geography, pantomime
- Interpersonal—brainstorming, personality profile, different opinions
- Intrapersonal—promoting wondering, thinking before you start
- Logical-mathematical—puzzles and patterns, predicting and testing
- Verbal-linguistic—creating words, puns, freewriting for thinking
- Naturalist—comparing/contrasting, displays and scrapbooks

1081-W . . . $30

Increase your potential with the powerful combination of information, inspiration, and practical activities

THE RE-ENCHANTMENT OF LEARNING
A Manual for Teacher Renewal and Classroom Transformation
by Sam Crowell, Ed.D., Renate Nummela Caine, Ph.D., and Geoffrey Caine, LL.M.
Professional Development

Boost your effectiveness in meeting today's challenges with strategies based on the new sciences. Applications of these field-tested methods have resulted in higher student grades and test scores. And more importantly, dramatic transformations are evidenced by—

- Personal lives taking on a renewed sense of meaning
- Administrators focusing on bringing out the best in everyone
- Students taking pride in their work, behavior, and classrooms

1082-W . . . $32

Order Form

Call, Write, or FAX for your FREE Catalog!

Qty.	Item #	Title	Unit Price	Total
	1081-W	Multiple Intelligences Made Easy	$30	
	1082-W	The Re-Enchantment of Learning	$32	

Name _____
Address _____
City _____
State _____ Zip _____
Phone (_____) _____
E-mail _____

Subtotal
Sales Tax (AZ residents, 5%)
S & H (10% of Subtotal, min. $4.00)
Total (U.S. Funds only)

CANADA: add 22% for S& H and G.S.T.

Method of payment (check one):
❑ Check or Money Order ❑ Visa
❑ MasterCard ❑ Purchase Order Attached
Credit Card No. _____
Expires _____
Signature _____

100% SATISFACTION GUARANTEE

Upon receiving your order you'll have 90 days of risk-free evaluation. If you are not 100% satisfied, return your order in saleable condition within 90 days for a 100% refund of the purchase price. No questions asked!

To order write or call:
P.O. Box 66006-W
Tucson, AZ 85728-6006
1-800-232-2187
FAX 520-323-9402
http://www.zephyrpress.com

Zephyr Press, Inc.®
REACHING THEIR HIGHEST POTENTIAL